Strategic Connections

The New Face of Networking in a Collaborative World

Anne Baber, Lynne Waymon,
André Alphonso, and Jim Wylde

AMACOM AMERICAN MANAGEMENT ASSOCIATION

New York • Atlanta • Brussels • Chicago • Mexico City • San Francisco
Shanghai • Tokyo • Toronto • Washington, D. C.

Bulk discounts available. For details visit: www.amacombooks.org/go/specialsales
Or contact special sales: Phone: 800-250-5308 / Email: specialsls@amanet.org
View all the AMACOM titles at: www.amacombooks.org
American Management Association: www.amanet.org

Library of Congress Cataloging-in-Publication Data

Baber, Anne
Strategic connections : the new face of networking in a collaborative world / Anne Baber, Lynne Waymon, André Alphonso, and Jim Wylde.
    pages cm
Includes bibliographical references and index.
ISBN 978-0-8144-3496-3 (hardcover : alk. paper) — ISBN 0-8144-3496-7 (hardcover : alk. paper) — ISBN 978-0-8144-3497-0 (ebook) 1. Business communication. 2. Interpersonal communication. 3. Business networks. I. Title.
HF5718.B333 2015
650.1'3—dc23

2014026198

About AMA

American Management Association (www.amanet.org) is a world leader in talent development, advancing the skills of individuals to drive business success. Our mission is to support the goals of individuals and organizations through a complete range of products and services, including classroom and virtual seminars, webcasts, webinars, podcasts, conferences, corporate and government solutions, business books, and research. AMA's approach to improving performance combines experiential learning—learning through doing—with opportunities for ongoing professional growth at every step of one's career journey.

Printing number
10 9 8 7 6 5 4 3 2 1

To Todd, a real Renaissance man: The day you joined the company was our lucky day. You've got it all—the creative spark, the technical smarts, and the generous heart. Our deepest thanks for your superlative support and positive touch all along the way. And for the Scrabble games in between all the work, too.

—Anne and Lynne

CONTENTS

6 Deepen Interactions / 133

7 Communicate Expertise / 157

8 Create New Value / 179

PREFACE
The Overwhelming
Case for Face to Face

Here's the challenge: Network with a new purpose, collaborate in ways you never have before, and impact your organization. A new paradigm is emerging, a paradigm we call the *Network-Oriented Workplace.*

In the new workplace, whether you're a CEO or an employee, you have a new role to play—and new opportunities for contributing to your organization's success. *Strategic Connections* shows you how to commit to this new networker identity.

But, to become a player in the new environment, you'll need more than the mindset. You'll need to master advanced face-to-face skills. What's the value of face to face? Trust. Without trust, the collaboration needed to excel in today's environment is very unlikely.

We know something about this topic. Since 1990, we've been talking about, thinking about, and training people in face-to-face networking. A wide variety of corporate, academic, and government organizations have been not only our clients, but also our proving ground for the state-of-the-art tools and techniques presented in this, our eighth, book.

The Way to Collaboration

Figure P–1, The Big Picture, depicts the only route to collaboration. There are no shortcuts. Start reading at the bottom and work your way up. Equipped with The 8 Competencies for the Network-Oriented Workplace (see Figure P–2), you can move along to teach

FIGURE P–1. *The Big Picture*

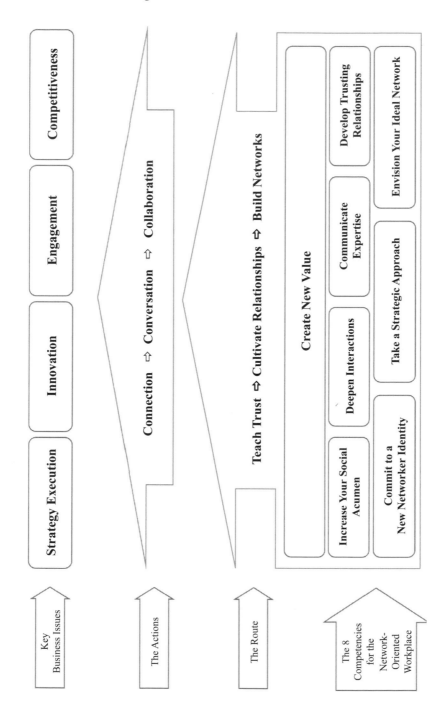

your contacts, both inside and outside the organization, to trust you. With trust, you can advance to relationships that are more productive and useful. As these relationships progress, your networks are energized. With your networking contacts, you connect, converse, and ultimately collaborate. (Many leaders assume—and it's a huge misconception—that most people instinctively know how to take these steps and that there are no skills that can speed you onward. Those assumptions simply are not true.)

Chapters 1 through 8 are devoted to helping you acquire each of these competencies, and each chapter is filled with examples, tips, tools, strategies, and stories to help you learn. Mastering these skills will assure that you're able to use networking to make the strategic connections you need to achieve your goals at work, in your career, and for the wider organization.

Make an Impact

In the new Network-Oriented Workplace, you direct your networking efforts to impact the big organizational issues.

- Your collaboration impacts *strategy execution*, speeding responsiveness and improving productivity.

- Your collaboration impacts *innovation*, prompting more risk taking, thinking outside the box, and experimenting.

- Your collaboration impacts *engagement*, raising satisfaction and eliciting your best.

- Your collaboration impacts *competitiveness*, streamlining processes, bringing in the business, and keeping and expanding the current client base.

This book is your guide for creating your success, as well as contributing to the success of your organization, by developing the networking skills that drive 21st-century collaborative workplaces.

—Anne Baber, Lynne Waymon,
André Alphonso, and Jim Wylde

FIGURE P-2. *The 8 Competencies for the Network-Oriented Workplace*

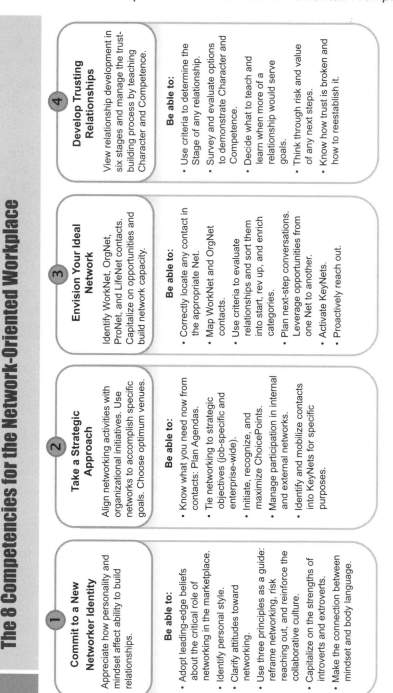

The 8 Competencies for the Network-Oriented Workplace

1 Commit to a New Networker Identity

Appreciate how personality and mindset affect ability to build relationships.

Be able to:

- Adopt leading-edge beliefs about the critical role of networking in the marketplace.
- Identify personal style.
- Clarify attitudes toward networking.
- Use three principles as a guide: reframe networking, risk reaching out, and reinforce the collaborative culture.
- Capitalize on the strengths of introverts and extroverts.
- Make the connection between mindset and body language.

2 Take a Strategic Approach

Align networking activities with organizational initiatives. Use networks to accomplish specific goals. Choose optimum venues.

Be able to:

- Know what you need now from contacts: Plan Agendas.
- Tie networking to strategic objectives (job-specific and enterprise-wide).
- Initiate, recognize, and maximize ChoicePoints.
- Manage participation in internal and external networks.
- Identify and mobilize contacts into KeyNets for specific purposes.

3 Envision Your Ideal Network

Identify WorkNet, OrgNet, ProNet, and LifeNet contacts. Capitalize on opportunities and build network capacity.

Be able to:

- Correctly locate any contact in the appropriate Net.
- Map WorkNet and OrgNet contacts.
- Use criteria to evaluate relationships and sort them into start, rev up, and enrich categories.
- Plan next-step conversations. Leverage opportunities from one Net to another.
- Activate KeyNets.
- Proactively reach out.

4 Develop Trusting Relationships

View relationship development in six stages and manage the trust-building process by teaching Character and Competence.

Be able to:

- Use criteria to determine the Stage of any relationship.
- Survey and evaluate options to demonstrate Character and Competence.
- Decide what to teach and learn when more of a relationship would serve goals.
- Think through risk and value of any next steps.
- Know how trust is broken and how to reestablish it.

The 8 Competencies for the Network-Oriented Workplace

5 — Increase Your Social Acumen

Be more confident and professional by mastering relationship rituals and understanding the elements of likeability.

Be able to:

- Make your name memorable and learn names using specific techniques.
- Deal with forgotten names.
- Easily join groups of people who are already talking.
- Use specific methods to end conversations with the future in mind.
- Apply tools and behaviors that increase the likelihood of likeability.
- Handle awkward moments.

6 — Deepen Interactions

Spark rich conversation to build and sustain relationships.

Be able to:

- Listen generously with a bias toward action.
- Show an active interest in the needs and perspectives of others.
- Ask questions designed to learn about others.
- Use questions to uncover needs and commonalities.
- Explore "iceberg" statements.
- Look for "the Give."
- Reconnect, follow through, and stay in touch.

7 — Communicate Expertise

Use examples and stories to teach contacts about organizational, team, and individual expertise, talents, experience, and interests.

Be able to:

- Answer "What do you do?" in a way that makes expertise visible and memorable.
- Call to mind, identify, and tell about events and successes that teach organizational, team, and individual capabilities.
- Use guidelines to construct and edit stories that highlight what you want to teach.
- Recognize storytelling opportunities.
- Deliver stories in a way that increases personal and organizational visibility.

8 — Create New Value

Employ networking tools and strategies to contribute to enterprise-wide success.

Be able to:

- Commit to collaborative problem-solving.
- Connect people and give access to resources, talent, and expertise.
- Be known for the BringBack you gather and distribute to colleagues.
- Use face-to-face networking skills with social media.
- Build a diverse network (gender, age, race, rank, function, geography, culture).
- Mentor others and model what you want to encourage.

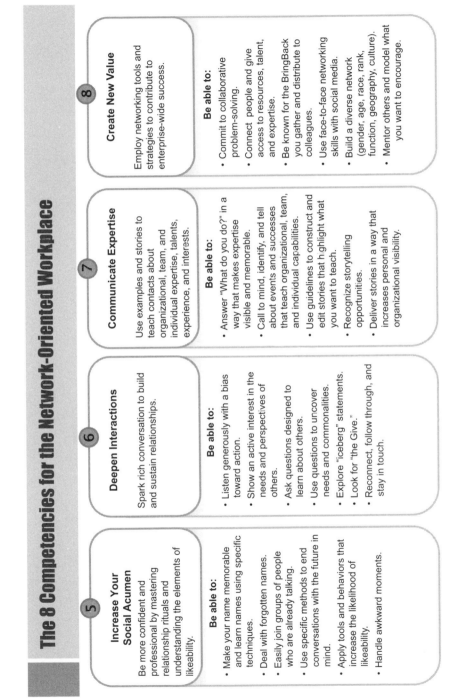

·······················

Introduction

The Eight Must-Have Skills
for Strategic Connections

NETWORKING IS recognized as a professional competency you
need no matter where you work, what your job title, or what your
level. As the Network-Oriented Workplace emerges, you will be
called on to use the power of your networks in a new way—to influence and impact the growth and success of your organization.

Strategic Connections helps you answer questions like, "What does
this mean about the way I approach my job? How does this change
the way I build relationships and collaborate in the workplace?" Have
you heard the call for collaboration in your organization? If you
haven't yet, it's sure to come in the not-too-distant future.

"Interpersonal skills of collaboration" was ranked number 1 by 75
percent of the 1700 CEOs queried in IBM's 2012 Global CEO Study.
Their 2013 study reiterates the importance of collaboration.

What does this growing focus on collaboration mean for you?
What do you need to start doing, stop doing, or do better?

Strategic Connections gives you the answers—the skills and concepts you need for personal career success in the new collaborative workplace.

What's the Back Story?

What has caused organizations to recognize the value of your networks? Old ideas about how the business world operates are giving way to new ways of working.

THEN	NOW
Command/Control	Participatory
Protecting Ideas	Spreading Ideas
Hierarchies/Silos	No Boundaries
Individual Effort	Collaboration
Quantity of Relationships	Quality of Trust

FIGURE I-1. Then and Now

The proliferation of the technologies for communicating has resulted in "power to the people" and is largely responsible for ending the command-and-control mentality of organizations. Replacing that old military model are openness and transparency. In today's complex and hyperconnected environment, your interpersonal skills of collaboration become the foundation of organizational success. Instead of focusing on running their organizations, CEOs must now focus on letting their organizations run. And the way organizations run, it turns out, isn't depicted by the organization chart.

"Although in the past, network performance behaviors have been seen as admirable but not required for employees—and leaders—they are becoming essential to success, as they reflect how work gets done in the new work environment," says a 2013 Corporate Executive Board publication, "The Rise of the Network Leader."

What are these "network performance behaviors" that have become so essential? The 8 Competencies for the Network-Oriented Workplace include everything you need to know to establish the trusting relationships necessary for collaboration. The 8 Competencies are the "interpersonal skills of collaboration" CEOs want. These skills are anchored in trust and activated through what's traditionally been called networking. The value of these face-to-face relationship-building skills has never been higher. They are one of the essential professional skill sets for the 21st century.

To take collaboration off the CEOs wish list and make it "the way we do things around here," you need a thorough understanding of a new kind of networking. That's what you'll get from *Strategic Connections*.

You'll soon be—if you haven't already been—(in the words of that IBM Study) "encouraged and empowered to develop a diverse and extensive network of contacts."

Of course, if you know anybody at work or in the world, you already have networks. Until recently, network building has happened without much encouragement from organizations. In fact, often organizations have policies and procedures that discourage networking. Calling for collaboration without addressing these barriers is counterproductive. It will take companies a while to synchronize the systems and develop a support structure for the Network-Oriented Workplace. There are a lot of things companies need to do to make it easier for your networks to flourish. Our ideas on this topic appear in Chapter 9.

But all the barriers aren't out there in the organization. Contacts Count's research indicates that only 20 percent of employees are networking at anywhere near their potential. If you are one of these "natural networkers," you are good at building relationships and believe in the value of networking. The remaining 80 percent of employees have beliefs that keep them from being the best they could be. If you're in this group, you need not only the skills embodied in The 8 Competencies, but also a new mindset. Asking you to collaborate without giving you the tools is, again, counterproductive. In the new work environment, everyone will need to develop networking capabilities. Even the 20 percent who are the best at networking have a lot to learn.

Why Put Face to Face Out Front?

In recent years, most organizations have invested heavily in people-connecting technologies. Thanks to technology, your ability to connect is a given. You can reach out to anyone with the tap of a finger. You reap the benefits of instant 24/7 access and vast stores of online information at your fingertips. But, what's just as important is your ability to forge face-to-face relationships both inside and outside your organization.

Our advice: Take a blended approach. Although this book teaches the skills of face-to-face networking, these same skills will enhance your ability to build relationships electronically. Electronic and face-to-face modes can do more than coexist: You have unprecedented opportunities to incorporate technology into your close contact networking for maximum effectiveness. When you reach out via technology, the use of these trust-building tools and techniques takes you beyond connection to relationship.

Make judicious use of all the technologies for connecting—but also realize their limitations. Having the ability to access fellow employees' profiles on LinkedIn, for example, is useful, but having a list of someone's interests and expertise is not the same as having a relationship.

"People with extensive face-to-face networks are roughly twice as productive as people who keep to themselves or only communicate over email," says Ben Waber. He's CEO of Sociometric Solutions, a management consulting firm that uses sensor ID badges to measure workplace interaction. He's also a senior researcher at Harvard Business School and a visiting scientist at the Massachusetts Institute of Technology's Media Lab. "Face-to-face interaction accounts for nearly all boosts in job satisfaction, while email communication has no effect," he also points out in "Forget the Office: Let Employees Work from Home," on BusinessWeek.com. Both productivity and job satisfaction are powerful reasons to choose face-to-face networking when you can. That's the way to build trusting relationships faster and more easily. That's what will pay off for you (and for your organization).

What Are the Benefits?

Your advanced networking skills will open up opportunities for you to:

- Make sure your talents and expertise get used and your ideas get heard.

- Impact the big issues your organization is grappling with.

- Feel more energized, satisfied, and engaged.

- Advance your career.

As your networking expertise expands, you can influence your organization's evolution into a Network-Oriented Workplace. You'll be able to accomplish not only your organization's initiatives, but also your own career goals. It's obvious that as your organization prospers, so do you. Networking used to be seen as a "soft skill." As you learn how to align your networking to the big goals of your organization, these skills become not just "nice to have," but "must-haves."

Look at these brief overviews of The 8 Competencies. You'll get an idea of the scope of these skills and what you can do with them.

COMPETENCY #1: COMMIT TO A NEW NETWORKER IDENTITY

Taking on the role of a strategic networker may be easy for you or it may be a huge change. As you become comfortable with that role, you will:

- Rid yourself of any misconceptions and outdated ideas about networking.

- Believe that networking is valuable and that you can learn to do it.

- Analyze your attitudes towards networking and recognize any reluctance that might hold you back. Take charge of managing your mindset.

- Learn techniques to make networking less stressful.

COMPETENCY #2: TAKE A STRATEGIC APPROACH

Goal setting, planning, and evaluating help you avoid the haphazard, scattershot, passive networking that wastes time. As you set goals, you will:

- Create the networking road maps for success.

- Construct Agendas that make even random, hallway conversations valuable.

- Choose the right networking groups to join and know exactly how to make the most of them.

- Put together comprehensive networking projects.

COMPETENCY #3: ENVISION YOUR IDEAL NETWORK

Having a clear picture of your networks—your WorkNet, OrgNet, ProNet, and LifeNet—means that you can spot both opportunities and deficiencies. As you clarify your mental image of your Four Nets, you will:

- Strengthen them, fill in the holes, and learn how to leverage contacts.

- Experience the power of pulling together a KeyNet to help you accomplish a specific project.

- Know how to enrich, rev up/start, and repair relationships.

- Build high-functioning and balanced networks that are even more valuable to your success and well-being.

COMPETENCY #4: DEVELOP TRUSTING RELATIONSHIPS

Trust is all-important, in networking as in life. When you know how to establish trust, you will be able to collaborate in more meaningful ways. You will:

- See how relationships intensify through six Stages of Trust.

- Know how to teach people about your Character and Competence—the two building blocks of trust.

- Understand the criteria for determining what Stage of Trust you've reached with any contact.

- Be able to plan the next steps to help that relationships evolve.

COMPETENCY #5: INCREASE YOUR SOCIAL ACUMEN

You can feel more comfortable, competent, and professional in all kinds of networking situations. You will:

- Have tried-and-true methods for remembering names, teaching your name, and joining groups.

- End conversations graciously and professionally.

- Boost your likeability, so others will seek you out and want to include you in their networks or participate in yours.

- Avoid awkward moments.

COMPETENCY #6: DEEPEN INTERACTIONS

Conversation isn't something you learned in school. You will:

- Ask questions and explore "iceberg statements" to find out about your contacts' expertise, as well as their Character and Competence, so that relationships can move forward.

- Discover how to listen for the right things.

- Look for "the Give" to position yourself as a "go-to person."

- Use a variety of techniques for following up to maintain and intensify relationships over time, so they become even more valuable.

COMPETENCY #7: COMMUNICATE EXPERTISE

Telling stories builds relationships. You can showcase your expertise . . . without bragging. You will:

- Answer "What do you do?" in a way that begins to establish your Character and Competence, directs the conversation to topics you care about, and makes you visible and memorable.

- Find the stories that best teach your contacts about your organization's, your team's, or your own expertise, experience, and interests.

- Craft stories that stick in people's minds and make you stand out so that opportunities find you.

COMPETENCY #8: CREATE NEW VALUE

Using networking skills, you can increase your contribution to and impact on your organization. You will:

- Have a new understanding of collaboration.

- Reframe networking.

- Risk reaching out.

- Boost your BringBack.

- Reinforce the collaborative culture.

- Put the tools of networking to work to benefit your organization as well as yourself.

How to Use This Book

Dog-ear the pages, highlight it, mark it up, write in the margins, use sticky notes and tabs. Talk about the ideas with your colleagues. Argue with us. Jot down your own examples and make note of your own experiences.

Work through it. Have paper and pen handy—or your laptop or tablet. Take these skills off the pages and make them your own. Draft several answers to that inevitable question, "What do you do?" Yes, you'll have multiple answers—not just one—so you can relate to the various individuals you meet. Your answers won't just recite the information on your business card. They'll provide bridges to topics you want to talk about and begin to teach your conversation partner what to come to you for. Work on your stories—most need a lot of editing—so they make your point without losing your listener in a morass of extraneous details.

Start anywhere. Although there's a logic to the order of The 8 Competencies, you can open this book to any page and learn a specific skill or grab a new idea about how to use your networks. You can customize *what* you learn and *how* you learn to serve your own needs at the moment. Of course, all the skills are important and useful. As you take all of them in, you'll be able to accomplish more with your networks.

1

....

Commit to a New Networker Identity

Strategic Connections: Explore Opportunities

At one Ohio-based high-tech company, 35 consulting engineers spent every day at client sites. These engineers were told that one-third of their annual bonuses would be based on finding new or expanded work from these clients. Only three engineers came through. The other 32? Even with a substantial financial incentive dangling in front of them, they couldn't and didn't.

WHAT DID THE three engineers who took their bonuses to the bank have that the others didn't? A robust and positive networker identity. Imagine them saying to themselves, "Yeah, I can see myself having those kinds of conversations with my client to explore new ways our firm might be of service."

Everybody has a networker identity. In this chapter, you'll learn how to expand and strengthen yours so you can participate fully in the emerging Network-Oriented Workplace. As you analyze your attitudes, you'll let go of misconceptions and outdated notions about networking. As you redefine networking, you'll adopt new ideas and beliefs to build a solid foundation for your new role. As you manage your mindset, you'll make sure nothing will hold you back as you begin to update and expand your repertoire of networking skills.

Analyze Your Attitudes

What's your current networker identity? To discover it, look through the list of comments below. Do you find one or more that you might give in answer to this question: "How do you feel about networking?"

- "Networking comes easy for me. I've always done it, and I enjoy it."

- "I was raised in a culture that frowns on talking about oneself. I'm not comfortable with taking credit for my achievements."

- "I'm shy. Talking with strangers or even people I know is difficult."

- "Isn't face to face rather old-fashioned? I'd rather connect electronically."

- "I do my job. Why should I have to promote myself?"

- "I know networking's important, but I don't have the time."

- "I have to network for my job, so I've found role models and picked up some ideas. I'm sure there's more to learn."

> *Some 80 percent of people have beliefs that hold them back.*

Those answers indicate the range of attitudes we see among employees. Our Contacts Count surveys show that only 20 percent of people are proficient networkers. If you're in this group, networking comes naturally to you, or you've figured out how to do it. Your attitude is positive, and committing to a new networker identity will be an easy transition for you. The remaining 80 percent of people have beliefs about networking that keep them from doing it well—or at all. If you're in this group, your attitude as you begin reading this book might be negative, or neutral, or fairly positive. Know that, wherever you are starting from, you can, if you keep an open mind, find your own networker identity that feels authentic and will help you succeed in the 21st-century Network-Oriented Workplace.

The Nine Biggest Misconceptions About Networking

The beliefs expressed here can prevent you from taking on your new networker identity. If you recognize yourself in any of these examples, think carefully about whether you want to hold on to a belief that limits your ability to learn and use the state-of-the-art skills presented in this book.

1. *"I'm a CPA, I shouldn't have to network,"* says Manny. "My work should stand for itself."

"The hardest people to get to network are scientists, engineers, and financial types," say researchers Rob Cross, Andrew Hargadon, and Salvatore Parise in their 2008 Network Roundtable publication, "Critical Connections: Driving Rapid Innovation with a Network Perspective." Some people have chosen what we call "quiet careers" that haven't in the past required much interaction. But the workplace is changing: Today, individual contributors become collaborators. If you have a professional identity that does not include "networker," it's time to update your definition of yourself.

2. *"I'm a professional engineer (architect, CPA, doctor, etc.),"* says Andie. "I'm not in sales."

Many organizations have now decided that "business development is everybody's business." That's what the engineers in this chapter's opening story found out when they were asked to talk with clients about expanding their engagements. In the new workplace, everyone takes ownership of the organization's success and that includes bringing in the business, whatever your job title.

3. *"I rarely get anything out of networking events,"* says Mel, a purchasing manager, "so, I've quit going."

In one Contacts Count study, more than 85 percent of people who attended a networking event said they hadn't come looking for anything in particular. As the saying goes, "If you aim at nothing, you'll hit it." If Mel had gone with goals in mind, he'd have a good chance to find what he was looking for. Skilled networkers make events pay off. And, of course, networking doesn't just happen at networking events; in the Network-Oriented Workplace, networking happens all during the workday—and beyond.

4. *"If I ask for help, won't I seem incompetent?"* asks Liz, a budget analyst. "I don't like the feeling of owing people."

Asking for help results in better decisions and outputs; giving help results in higher job satisfaction. There's no downside in those outcomes. "Everyone's work is improved by a dynamic process of seeking and giving feedback, ideas, and assistance," say Teresa Amabile, Colin M. Fisher, and Julianna Pillemar, authors of "IDEO's Culture of Helping," a 2014 article in the *Harvard Business Review*. Liz is stuck in a tit-for-tat notion of networking: You give me something, I owe you something back. But in the Network-Oriented Workplace, networkers don't keep score; they give generously.

• •

In the Network-Oriented Workplace, networkers give generously.

• •

5. *"If I'm networking, people will think I'm job-hunting,"* says Ernesto, an IT supervisor.

Networking was once pigeonholed as a job-seeking/career-advancing tool. But it's much more than that. The new environment encourages people to network not just for their own benefit, but also for the benefit of their organizations.

6. *"Networking is manipulative,"* says Teresa, a project manager. "I don't like the idea of arm-twisting someone to get him to do something for me."

In reality, that kind of approach to networking doesn't work anyway. Subterfuge, indirection, and pushiness don't get results. Those actions repel people rather than attract them. The best networkers teach their contacts to trust them. The trust-building process eliminates any hint of manipulation.

7. *"Networking is just schmoozing,"* says Karla, a manager of administrative services. "It's boring and . . . uncomfortable."

Strategic networkers sidestep superficialities and get down to business. They go beyond chitchat into conversations that can help them solve problems, come up with new ideas, and access valuable resources.

8. *"I'm an introvert. I'll never be a networker,"* says Kyle, a manager in corporate planning.

The experts agree: Slightly over half of us are introverts. And often introverts find interacting overstimulating and energy-draining. But they have the edge when it comes to planning and listening—two qualities that are very important in building relationships. And they especially appreciate the detailed, step-by-step instructions we give for the skills in The 8 Competencies. In a Network-Oriented Workplace, we'd expect half of the employees to be introverts *and* capable networkers.

9. *"I don't need face-to-face skills,"* says Lee. "Meeting with people is a waste of time. I just zap out an email or text message."

Why take an either/or approach? Why not use both? There's no doubt that people build trust faster when they're face to face. That's why strategic connectors choose in-person networking when they can.

Once you're rid of beliefs that hold you back, you can replace them with new beliefs that help you move forward.

The Definition of Networking

If you had to define networking, what would you say? Here's our definition:

> Networking is the deliberate and discretionary process of creating, cultivating, and capitalizing on trust-based, mutually beneficial relationships for individual and organizational success.

Note that networking:

- Is a process that takes time and intention.
- Involves initiating, maintaining, and making use of relationships.
- Is based on trust and benefits both parties.
- Impacts your results—and your organization's as well.

Once you understand this definition, use it in your belief system. These three beliefs are all you need:

1. Networking is valuable—to me and to my organization.

2. It can be learned.

3. I can learn it.

Believing in the value of networking shouldn't be a stretch. You'll find a wealth of examples of the benefits throughout this book. Look for examples that show the value of networking in getting your job done, in advancing your career, and in contributing to the success of your organization. Notice, too, the mounting evidence that organizations are recognizing the value of face-to-face networking and will be more and more supportive of your efforts.

Believing that networking is a set of skills you can master is also easy. The 8 Competencies include everything you need to know to create, cultivate, and capitalize on relationships.

Believing that you can learn these skills comes as you shed self-imposed restrictions and misguided misconceptions. Throw away any remaining remnants of reluctance that you notice when you catch yourself thinking, "I can't be an expert networker because . . . ."

Become a Strategic Networker

If you're ready to expand your networking horizons, you're on your way to becoming a strategic networker by:

- Choosing your mindset/beliefs (you've begun this process by buying this book).

- Learning a wide range of skills.

- Making strategic networker who you are and how you operate.

Make strategic networker who you are and how you operate.

Imagine your life as a strategic networker. You believe in the power of networking to help accomplish your—and your organization's—goals. As you move from individual contributor to collaborator, you make a bigger impact on your organization's success. You understand the steps in the trust-building process and choose face-to-face interactions over electronic ones whenever possible. Because you've mastered the state-of-the-art network-building skills, you feel comfortable, confident, and professional as you develop and leverage your networks. You are able to adapt these face-to-face skills to build trust with your at-a-distance contacts. ou add strategic networker to your self-concept. When dealing with a problem or challenge or project, you immediately think, "Who do I know (or who could I know) who could/should be involved or who might help with this?" Your specific job is fresh and exciting as you find ways to involve others and align your work with desired organizational outcomes.

On a more personal level, with your new networking expertise you connect in richer ways with family, friends, and your larger community.

Seeing the Possibilities

"All those casual conversations—I began to see the possibilities. At Thanksgiving dinner, talking with my uncle, I realized he could be a referral source. At the IT security specialists' network, a guy I know well was looking for a new job, and I told him about an opening at our firm. At my alumni group, I got to know a partner in a real estate development company that builds schools and hospitals and offered to introduce her to our partner who specializes in that.

"I get it now. My job is to promote the firm and help my coworkers—no matter what their job titles—find the people and resources they need to get the job done. I'm beginning to get comfortable with my new networker identity: I'm an IT manager *and* a networker."

Activate Your Networker Identity

As you use the skills in The 8 Competencies to activate your new networker identity, you'll be faced with many decisions and opportunities. Let these three principles drive your responses:

1. Reframe networking.

2. Risk reaching out.

3. Reinforce the collaborative culture.

REFRAME NETWORKING

In the past, many people had a self-serving approach to networking; they saw interacting as the way to get something for themselves. There's nothing wrong with wanting your efforts to bear fruit. But that's only part of the story. Networking is not just about talking and taking; it's about teaching and giving.

* *

Reframe networking as teaching and giving.

* *

When you reframe networking to include teaching, you'll immediately feel more comfortable and professional. With a teaching mindset, you put aside any sense of manipulating people and focus instead on providing useful information about yourself and your organization. If you've thought of yourself as shy or introverted or bound by cultural prohibitions, you'll feel liberated as you begin to think of networking as teaching. The other side of teaching is learning. Deciding to learn about others also feels easy and energizing. As you master the skills in The 8 Competencies, you'll discover many ways to teach about yourself and learn about your contacts.

When you reframe networking to also include giving, you may initially feel some reluctance or apprehension. You might worry that you'll be taken advantage of or that you don't have anything to give. You may be used to thinking of networking as an equal exchange: I give; I get. You can go beyond the idea that networking is trading. Move into a "give first, give freely" mindset. Giving generously aids the trust-building process and enhances your likeability. Your willingness and ability to give are aspects of your networker identity. As you give, you help to create the giving culture that characterizes the Network-Oriented Workplace and sets it apart from the old command-and-control system. That old system put you into competition with your coworkers; the new Network-Oriented Workplace draws you into collaboration for mutual success.

RISK REACHING OUT

How did reaching out to another human being become something that feels scary? Analyze your apprehensions about connecting. When you feel that attack of nerves that alerts you to a risky situation, take a look at your fears. You may decide that your concerns are quite silly. Feeling reluctant to join a group of people who are talking with each other? Does that experience tap into a long ago, high-school-age angst about being excluded from the in-group? How to overcome this? Catastrophize. Ask yourself, "What's the worst thing that could happen?" Many fears about interacting can be quashed with a good dose of reality. Prepare and practice. Certainly, after you have internalized all of the skills in The 8 Competencies, you'll feel well equipped for your networking adventures. Having the skills reduces the risk. As you build trusting relationships, risk diminishes. In those relationships, others have your back and will go to bat for you. As trust grows, you'll be more willing to take risks, think out of the box, and innovate. Be brave. Dare, act, go boldly, take the first step. Risk reaching out!

REINFORCE THE COLLABORATIVE CULTURE

In the past, networking at work has been undervalued, unappreciated, and underutilized. Now organizations are beginning to value, appreciate, and recognize the power of your networks. Any new idea needs its champions. Become a champion for the Network-Oriented Workplace.

To put this principle into action, advocate for best networking practices. Act as a networking role model whenever you can. Mentor and teach networking concepts and skills to younger workers and new hires. As you participate in the Network-Oriented Workplace, you reinforce the collaborative culture.

Manage Your Mindset

You've analyzed your attitudes, off-loaded debilitating ideas, and begun to establish your strategic networker belief system. But you still may have some negative images lurking about in the nooks and crannies of your mind. What can you do to knock out negativity, energize yourself, and transform yourself from an "I can't . . ." to an "I can . . ." networker? Use these tips, tools, and techniques to take charge of your mindset.

WATCH YOUR LANGUAGE

There's no denying that the term *networking* has, through the years, collected some negative connotations. Several common comments give networking a chilly aura. Brrr! People say:

"He gave me the cold shoulder."

"What can I say to break the ice?"

"I hate to make cold calls."

"I got cold feet when I thought about going to the meeting alone."

"I just froze up."

It's hard to feel excited about making contact when your mind is full of pictures like these. If you think of other people—people you might network with—as cold and rejecting, it will be hard for you to enjoy the moment, exchange information, or explore future opportunities. When you hear yourself thinking or making any of these comments, reject these images and come in from the cold.

Some of the other words and phrases people use when they are talking about networking devalue and demean networking. Here's our list of the top 10 turnoffs in the language of networking and why we don't like them.

1. "Schmoozing." That word can make networking conversations seem unimportant and worse, insincere!

2. "30-second commercial." Why refer to a hard sell when you're teaching someone what you do and trying to build trust?

3. "Pick your brain." Here are the vultures coming in for the carrion. We wish people would say, "I'd like to get your thoughts about something."

4. "Work a room." So depersonalizing and one-sided, this phrase sounds as if you intend to work people over and take all you can get from them.

5. "Elevator speech." This phrase diminishes the teaching and trust-building that could occur when you tell what you do.

6. "Tricks of the trade." Let's not imply anything that smacks of manipulation. There are no "tricks" in our approach to networking.

7. "Favor bank." Doing things for others is the right thing; just so they'll "owe me one" is the wrong reason. Give without strings, without expectations of getting—that's the way to create networks that work.

8. "Power lunch." Yes, invite a powerful contact to lunch, but don't call it that. It sounds too much as if you value people just for their positions.

9. "Business card exchange." Exchanging cards without building trust is nonproductive and makes only a "cardboard connection," not a real one. When you leave a networking event with 20 or 30 cards, what do you do with them? Put them in your database? Invite those people to link with you, even through you don't remember who most of them are? Toss 'em into the trash? Only exchange cards with people you have genuinely connected with.

10. "Important people." Don't you hate it when you are talking with someone and that person is looking over your shoulder

in search of someone better to talk with? Give your whole attention to the person you are with. Seek out contacts based on their expertise, not their titles.

CATCH YOUR CRITIC

You climb into your car to go to a networking event. You put your key in the ignition. You turn into the street . . . and all of a sudden, you're there. You have no recollection of the route you took, the traffic you coped with, or the signs and houses and businesses you passed.

You've been on autopilot. But, when you think about it, you remember that your Critic—the voice in your head—has been haranguing you.

The voice makes it very hard—sometimes impossible—for you to connect easily with others. Notice how your Critic sabotages you.

During introductions, the voice in your head taunts you. Just when the person you're talking with gives his name, the Critic yells, "You never can remember people's names." Sure enough, while the Critic is hollering, the other person's name is blotted out.

In the middle of a conversation, the Critic's voice mutters, "You never can think of anything to talk about." And guess what . . . a self-fulfilling prophecy . . . you aren't able to think of anything to say.

After you've been talking with someone for several minutes, the Critic's voice harangues, "This person would rather be talking to someone more important." And you fade out of the conversation, stammering something about needing to freshen your drink.

* *

Change your Critic into a Coach.

* *

The Critic is bad news. Your brain believes what you tell it about yourself. The good news is you can transform your Critic into a helpful Coach.

If you notice what your Critic says and don't like it, you can reprogram that voice in your head to give you positive and encouraging messages instead of negative and discouraging ones.

Teach the voice in your head to say something helpful and supportive. Whenever your Critic makes you feel uncomfortable and incapable, think of encouraging statements that make you feel confident and strong. Come up with the words that reflect your beliefs that networking is valuable and that you can do it well. Use statements like:

"This is going to be interesting."

"I'm well-prepared and eager to talk to people today."

"I wonder what great ideas and opportunities I can discover as
   I connect with these people."

Change the way you talk to yourself about your ability to network. Combine your new mindset with the specific skills in this book to become a confident, strategic networker.

BELIEVE THE BEST ABOUT YOURSELF AND OTHERS

Your beliefs about yourself and other people will help you succeed at connecting. Take Paul, for example. He used to be apprehensive about entertaining out-of-town clients at dinner. But, to cope with his reluctance about meeting new people, he's gotten in the habit of giving himself a pep talk. "I say to myself, 'They've got kids and hobbies and hopes and dreams just like I do.' I think about all the things we have in common. If I prepare myself like that, I'm okay."

Paul discovered through experience what psychologists have verified by studying the conversational patterns of people meeting for the first time. Numerous researchers have found that if people meeting for the first time believe they have a lot in common, they act very much as if they are old friends. They pay attention to subtle conversational cues and match each other's progress through the conversation. If one brings up a lighter, more informal topic, the other responds with a light topic of his own. If one says something self-revealing, the other follows.

On the other hand, if the strangers are told they have nothing in common, conversation limps along, and both parties feel they haven't connected. This research reinforces the idea that your attitude toward others impacts your success as a networker.

ENERGIZE YOURSELF

Brian, who works in IT, says, "I prepare myself to walk into a room full of people. In my spare time I play in a rock band, so I imagine my 'entrance music.' I hear my favorite song playing in my head, and it makes me feel upbeat, positive, and confident." Can't you just see him walking in with his head high and his smile bright? What's your entrance music?

No doubt about it, your body language sends a message to others. But Amy Cuddy, professor at the Harvard Business School, has determined that your body language sends a message not only to other people, but also to your own brain. Her research shows that if you change your body language, you can change the way you feel and behave. Taking a "power pose" for two minutes before you go to a networking event or give an important presentation or deal with a difficult person changes your hormone levels and actually makes you more confident and able to take risks. You can invent your own pose. You might clasp your hands behind your head and put your feet on your desk—the very picture of the powerful and confident CEO. Or you can spread your arms above your head, making a V for Victory, and take a wide stance. Your goal: Take up as much space as possible. A powerful pose is expansive and open. In contrast, a powerless pose is contracted and closed, hunched in with your arms touching your torso and your legs crossed. People have said, "Fake it 'til you make it." Using this technique, you can literally fake it 'til you *become* it.

You can watch Professor Cuddy's popular TED Talk, "Your Body Language Shapes Who You Are," for more information about her intriguing research.

FIND ROLE MODELS

Look for people who are comfortable and confident networkers and use them as role models. Find several people so that you get several points of view. It's said that imitation is the sincerest form of flattery. Don't be reluctant to let people know that you consider them good examples to follow. In fact, interview your role models to find out how they came by their expertise and what barriers they had to overcome. You may be surprised when they say they're shy or introverted. Role models can be good sounding boards and mentors as well as people whose behavior you mirror.

When one CPA firm wanted to instill the idea that business development is everyone's business, the partners took part in a panel discussion to share stories about their rainmaker activities. The younger employees were heartened and encouraged when they discovered that the partners weren't born with the "gift of gab," but had developed over many years the networking behaviors that helped them attract clients.

Your networker identity arises from your positive mindset and your mastery of networking skills. It's not about just changing your hat. It's not a mask. It's not a fake self that you put on when you go to a conference or meet with a prospect or work with colleagues on a project. It's not a performance or a technique. It's about making "networker" who you are, an authentic self-definition.

2

·····················

Take a Strategic
Approach

Strategic Connections: Raise Rainmakers

At a Florida CPA firm, the founders were worried. About to retire, they wanted be sure that the younger generation would be able to grow the firm in the future. "I want us to make client development and business networking part of our core professional develop-ment expectation," said one partner. Another said, "We've got to start training our folks early and raise some rainmakers. Reaching out, building referral relationships, and 'telling our story' don't come naturally to most CPAs. They need to know that business development is everybody's business. It's a way of life at our firm."

THESE CPAs aren't the only ones who are finding that networking has been added to their job descriptions. Being good at the tasks in your job description is no longer enough. In the new collaborative environment, every job is Job + N(etworking). Whether you want to use networking tools to bring in the business or want to grow strong internal and external networks that spark creativity and lead you to feel more engaged, it's time to professionalize your networking. The skills in Competency 2 will help you to overcome the biggest networking mistake people make—not being strategic.

In this chapter, you'll learn more about networking to get the job done, to support career advancement, and to help your organization create new value. You'll plan what you want to talk about, so that, whether you meet someone new in the cafeteria or see someone you know well at a networking event, you'll be ready—and not just say whatever pops into your head. You'll learn how to choose the networking groups that are right for you, and get visible. You'll be able to decide if the groups you've joined are bringing you the benefits you want. And you'll know how to take on big networking projects with big goals.

Networking in the Collaborative Culture

In this new, collaborative environment, your reasons for building deep and wide networks expand. Sure, you connect and collaborate to get your job done. Of course, a strong cadre of contacts will help you advance your career. And now, your organization is depending on you to use your contacts to create enterprise-wide benefits. Now you network not only for yourself, but also for your team, your department, and your whole organization.

* *

Be a proactive—not reactive—networker.

* *

Vow to be a proactive—not reactive—networker. For people in our workshops, it's an "aha moment" when they realize they have been just accepting the networking situations and opportunities that have come their way. Serendipity is great, but when you focus your networking on getting the job done, supporting organization-wide priorities, and enhancing your career, you'll accelerate and streamline making things happen.

Decide how to use your network, so you spend your time and energy well. You'll probably have many reasons to network. Do you want to:

- Uncork a bureaucratic bottleneck?

- Make progress on a project that's been sitting on your desk?

- Invent a new way of doing something?

- Pull together a group of people to solve an interdepartmental problem?

- Tackle a new assignment?

- Create a constant flow of referrals and new business?

- Launch a new program?

- Bring increased visibility or influence to your group or firm?

- Get the job of your dreams?

- Position yourself for a promotion?

Let's look more closely at the role networking plays with your job and your organizational and career goals.

JOB + N: GETTING THE JOB DONE

As futurist Faith Popcorn once said, "Whatever you need to know, the answer is probably *not* in your office." So one of the first things to ask yourself when you have a new project or responsibility is, "Do I know someone who might have a resource, an idea, or a contact to help me get this done?"

Pilar, a recruiter for a large engineering firm, needed to find summer interns and create a steady stream of candidates to fill entry-level positions. She reached out to the career placement specialists at several nearby universities in Montreal. One of the specialists at the university introduced her to Jacques, President of the Honor Society for Students in the Mechanical and Aerospace Programs. Jacques invited Pilar to be on a panel called "How to Succeed at Your Summer Internship." Pilar's firm also sponsored an event for the honor society, and she found that the more she got to know the career specialists, professors, and students, the easier it became to find and attract top-notch interns and job candidates.

Francesca's manager asked her to come up with a process their department could use to assess which prospective vendors had the most advanced environmentally friendly operations. She spent the better part of a day online and was overwhelmed by the amount of information she found. So she decided to make a list of people she knew in her own organization who might know something about the topic. The next day, she called and sent emails to a number of people in other departments and divisions. What she found out surprised her. Across the entire organization, she uncovered three task forces focusing on purchasing from environmentally responsible sources. She talked with her manager, and they decided to work on bringing the groups together. Francesca commented later, "Using my contacts to avoid reinventing the wheel was an eyeopener. I'll never start another project without first checking to see what's already in the works."

JOB + N: CONTRIBUTING TO ENTERPRISE-WIDE INITIATIVES

In the Network-Oriented Workplace, your reasons for building deep and wide networks expand beyond just getting your job done. No longer can you design your networks solely to serve your own purposes. Now you network not only for yourself, but also for your team, your department, and your whole organization.

An executive at a large Internet services company told us, "I want people to lift their eyes. I want them to look up from their desks and look laterally across the organization. I want them to pay more attention to how they can help with the larger issues. Our CEO wants us to double revenue in six years without incurring more costs. To make this happen people have to look at the big picture and take broader ownership of the business."

Another executive told us, "I want people to get out of their cubicles and find out how what they're doing can help or inform others in our organization. We're only 360 people, but we're not talking with each other enough."

It's your job to know what the big issues are and to figure out where and how you can contribute to them. Use the six questions below to explore your own organization's key goals.

It's your job to find the big issues and figure out how to contribute.

1. *What's up with my boss?* Periodically, have a conversation with your boss about her projects and challenges and find out what's coming down the pike. Scan your networks for contacts and resources that you might offer.

Linda knew that her manager was increasingly concerned about how to retain employees who'd been with the company from two to five years. When Linda attended a conference, she spotted a session on retaining younger workers and was able to bring back valuable ideas and contacts to pass along.

2. *What are the big goals?* Whether you work for an organization that has three employees or 300,000, you can bet that somebody has set some goals. Find them. They can sometimes sound quite inspiring, but vague: "Treat customers as we would like to be treated." Or they can be very down to earth: "Improve new employee retention rate by 10 percent." Some are general: "Improve customer service." Some are specific: "Decrease our backlog by 18 percent." Whatever they are, figure out how your work can impact them and how you can help.

Amira, the executive secretary to the county executive, noticed that her county had a huge influx of foreign-born residents. She knew the county's customer service goals would never be met if staffers couldn't speak the languages of the citizens they were trying to serve. She surveyed all 1800 employees to find out what languages each of them spoke and provided the list to every office. Then when someone speaking Pashto came in to get a contractor's license, for instance, he could quickly be matched up with a Pashto-speaking staffer.

3. *What's in the company news?* Review internal publications and newsletters. What is the CEO or agency head saying, either to internal or external audiences? What's new on the website? Do you have hidden talents or resources in your networks that might position you to contribute to initiatives or that would help you come up with an innovative approach where it's needed?

Clarence, in procurement, knew a lot about blogging with customers because of his special assignment in a previous job with another company. He reached out to Hugh, the new point person in charge of online customer contact initiatives, to offer his ideas and support.

4. *What's the scuttlebutt?* Make water-cooler conversations count. Ask your colleagues questions that explore trends and new initiatives. Say, "What do you think it'll mean for our department when the company opens the new office in San Francisco?" Or, "How do you think the new government regulations will affect our work?"

Greg heard through the grapevine that company leaders were talking about how to encourage healthier employee eating habits and lifestyles, so he offered to introduce someone he knew through his alumni association to the person in human resources who had been tasked with "the healthy project." Greg's contact was the executive chef at a farm-to-table restaurant in a nearby city. The chef consulted on new menus for the cafeteria featuring fresh foods, calorie information, and new, lower-calorie options.

5. *What's the industry intrigue?* Put on your sleuth's hat and find answers to questions like, "What are the industry movers and shakers saying? What do the pundits predict? What do experts say may make it harder for us to compete? Or easier? What changes will bring us a new kind of internal or external customer? What's going on in the world that will most certainly change the way we do business?" Read business and industry publications.

When Kiri became VP of operations for a small jewelry manufacturing company, she read about recent trends in online purchases. She tracked the growth of Valentine's Day gifts ordered online for the past six years. Based on those trends, she predicted that sales at her company could spike by as much as 12 percent in February. She was ready with a newly hired crew of part-time, short-term workers to fulfill orders.

6. *What's for lunch?* Offering food turns a meeting into a time for people to relax and get to know each other. Order in some sandwiches and invite people from one or two other departments to join you. Learn more about what they do and how your work interfaces with theirs. Who knows what problems might be solved or innovations might be dreamed up?

Klahan, in corporate communications, sometimes felt blindsided by requests he got from people in training. When his group was too busy to respond immediately, he worried that they would be seen as unresponsive. Over a couple of friendly, informal lunches, his five staffers and the training team of four got to know each other. They came up with an easy way to share their annual project calendars, so there would be no more surprises or last-minute requests.

When you use your networking skills to create enterprise-wide results, you become a leader, not just an employee, no matter where you are in the hierarchy.

JOB + N: CREATING YOUR CAREER

As one of our workshop participants said with a smile, "Hey, if I get my job done and help with all those wider goals, won't my career advancement just take care of itself?" Well, not exactly. Your career still needs special attention, a grand plan, mentors and sponsors, and people you've carefully educated to know the value you produce in the workplace.

Center for Talent Innovation CEO Sylvia Ann Hewlett in a May 2010 *Harvard Business Review* article recommends finding a sponsor, someone in a senior position who will introduce you to the right people and teach you "the secret language of success." Companies such as American Express, Deloitte, Citibank, and Cisco all have these kinds of programs to connect high-potential future leaders with top talent who will smooth the path to the C-suite. Don't leave your career to chance. Map out your steps to success just as you would for any other workplace project. No one knows better than you where you want to go next, what kind of work you enjoy most, and what types of new expertise you'd like to develop.

When one large defense contractor reorganizes or downsizes, people are told they must find a new internal position for themselves within two months or be laid off—a compelling reason to have built and maintained relationships across four geographically dispersed business units. It's always a good idea to target a couple of jobs you would like to have elsewhere in your organization and become known to the managers. Also, if those jobs require new skills, you can get a head start on acquiring them.

Use the skills in this book to get in the driver's seat and create opportunities that excite you. Most of us will get up and go to work for 10,000 days—or more. So why not make sure you're doing work you like, with people you enjoy, toward goals you care about?

Put Some Purpose in Your Small Talk

Is your small talk too small? Unfortunately, there's one conversation that everybody knows, word-for-word. It goes like this:

"Hi, how are you?"

"Not bad. How are you?"

"Not bad. What's new?"

"Not much. What's new with you?"

"Not much. Been real busy. . . ."

"Me too. Well, good to see you."

"Good to see you. We'll have to get together sometime."

"Great idea. I'll give you a call."

"Well, bye. See you later."

This is a conversation in search of a topic! Without a topic—or several—in mind that *you* want to talk about, you'll waste your time in purposeless chitchat like that "one-size-fits-all" conversation.

To be strategic, get ready to talk. You think about what to wear. You look up directions to wherever you're going. Why not plan ahead to have things to talk about? Have a conversation plan; it's vital to starting conversations and infusing them with some purpose and some pizzazz. As one client put it, "Oh, I get it . . . . You've got to be *prepared* to be spontaneous!"

> **Your Agenda is your list of topics you want to talk about.**

You can think of your conversation plan as your "networking Agenda," a word we are using with a very specific meaning. Your networking Agenda is a mental or written list of what you have To Give and what you want To Get. Having a networking Agenda energizes and empowers you, so that you'll benefit more from networking encounters. Using your Agenda will help you uncover the commonalities and needs that help trust grow. Keeping your

Agenda in mind, you'll feel comfortable and capable of enjoying yourself, making contact, gathering information, and seeking out opportunities. Since you have unique purposes, you will have a unique Agenda. Yours will reflect your background, your interests, your challenges, and your experiences, both in your personal life and in your work life.

Many people dread networking situations, in part because they wonder what to talk about. Actually, when it comes to topics, the problem is not that there's nothing to talk about. The problem is that there's *too much* to talk about! Hundreds of topics come crashing in on each of us every day via the Internet, newspaper, TV, radio, and junk mail. Often no one topic looks that much more interesting than any other. So it seems hard, maybe impossible, to select from all of the ideas racing around in your head. Having a networking Agenda simplifies the situation. And you automatically care about—and have energy for—the topics on your own Agenda list.

BEGIN WITH THE RIGHT SIDE

There are two sides to your Agenda; one labeled To Get and the other, To Give. Most people, as they think about networking, focus on "What's in it for me?" That's not the right place to begin. In fact, the second biggest mistake people make about networking (after not being strategic) is to think that networking is about getting. It's not about getting; it's about giving.

Giving—not taking—is the way to build your network. It's not just a nice thing to do; it's the *smart* thing to do. Psychologists have discovered a quirk of human nature that we call the Reciprocity Principle. It goes like this: If you give somebody something, he will try to give you something back. It gets even better. If you give somebody something, he will insist on giving you more than you gave him. Doesn't that sound exactly like what you want to happen when you're networking? To plug into the Reciprocity Principle, give first and give freely. You're actually in control of only half of the networking process—the giving part. So doesn't it make sense to lead with giving—something you control?

• •

The Reciprocity Principle: When you give, people will insist on giving you back even more.

• •

Keep at the top of your mind all you have to give, and give generously. Be helpful to others. Five years ago, an executive gave Ellen some career advice. This year, when she received the Employee of the Year Award from her company, she mentioned the executive in her acceptance speech, thanked him, and told how she felt inspired to mentor others because of his generosity early in her career.

WHAT DO YOU HAVE TO GIVE?

People often scratch their heads and say, "Give? I don't know what I have to give." To create your Give list, think about your accomplishments, skills, enthusiasms, interests, and resources. What are you so excited about that you'd talk to anybody, anywhere, anytime about it? Almost anything you are enthusiastic or knowledgeable about—in your professional life or in your leisure time—can become a good conversational topic. The things you have to give automatically become topics that help you connect with the people you meet. They also let people know what to count on you for. When there's a lull in the conversation or when people say, "What's new?" bring up a topic that's on your Give list.

Janice is an engineer who works for a large firm in New York City. Notice that her Give list includes both personal and professional topics:

- A great course on presentation skills

- The best deli in New York City

- Fund-raising ideas for nonprofit organizations (she volunteers for one!)

- Innovative ideas for streamlining proposals and bids

- Running webcasts as an alternative to in-person training

- Managing summer interns

If you wish you had more to give others, it may be a sign that you need to spice up your life. Do more. Experience more. Learn more. Risk more. Learn a new job skill. Volunteer with a group whose mission you admire. Take that exotic vacation you've been talking about.

WHAT WOULD YOU LIKE TO GET?

After you've thought through what you have to give, it's time to think about what you want to find, learn, create, connect with, understand, or know about. Just like your Give list, your Get list is also endless and ever-changing. To get in touch with what you'd like to get, look at your desk; look at your life. What problems are you trying to solve? What opportunities do you want to investigate? What are your upcoming challenges? What's one resource, person, idea, or bit of information that you'd celebrate finding? Once you have your list, see how each one of the items is a potential conversation starter.

Alan is a supply chain management director for a global manufacturing firm. He just moved to San Francisco. Here's his Get list:

- A buyer for my condo in Boston

- A good restaurant to take business guests to in Sydney next month

- Speakers for our annual vendor's conference

- More warehouse space for our plant in Costa Rica

- An easy way to practice my Spanish

Your Give and Get lists create your Agenda and guarantee that you'll have purposeful, strategic conversations. Don't leave home without it!

WHEN TO USE YOUR AGENDA

Make an Agenda before you go to networking events, but don't stop there. If you make an Agenda every day for 30 days, you will get used to coming up with items for your Give and Get lists. It will become automatic. Make it part of your breakfast routine. Take an index card and write your Give list on one side and your Get list on the other side. That way, you'll be ready for any conversation. There's always a bit of a risk in reaching out. You can make reaching out feel comfortable, instead of risky, by having an Agenda.

Plan your Agenda to get the most out of networking events.

Connect at ChoicePoints

Some conversations are more serendipitous and on the run. Every day you come to "ChoicePoints," opportunities to connect and converse that happen spontaneously. ChoicePoints are those moments when you can choose to reach out to someone—or not. You'll need your Agenda for these encounters also. To be a strategic connector, learn to recognize and respond to the chance meetings that happen every day. Think back over everything you did yesterday, every place you went, every person you saw. Do you take advantage of Choice-Points like these?

- You're standing in line with others waiting to enter the banquet at a conference.

- You're sitting at the table with others waiting for a training class, meeting, or workshop to begin.

- You're hammering nails with coworkers from all over the corporation at a Habitat for Humanity project.

- You see someone in the cafeteria you used to work with.

- You run into an old college friend at the health club.

. . . .

At ChoicePoints, you choose to reach out—or not.

. . . .

Of course, it may not always be convenient or even appropriate to reach out when someone crosses your path. You might be hurrying to get to a meeting on time. Or you might feel more comfortable doing some background research on someone you see at a monthly task force meeting before approaching her in the cafeteria. Even so, begin to notice how many opportunities for connection and conversation are right in front of you. What a great time to use your Agenda!

Here's how some people in our workshops have told us they used their Agendas and took the initiative to turn a ChoicePoint into a connection.

- Jim, a senior analyst, heard a couple of interns in the hall wondering where to go to lunch and invited them to join him.

- Leila stopped by Joan's office to learn more about the recent course she had taken on negotiating skills.

- Weng from the 12th floor rode the elevator down with Lou from the 10th floor and offered to give him a ride to the all-hands meeting across town, so they'd have time to talk.

- Anna made a point of sitting next to Virginia at the departmental meeting, so she could invite her to the next Women in Technology meeting.

As you add conversational skills to your repertoire, your comfort level in taking advantage of ChoicePoints will rise. Keeping your Gives and Gets in mind will make spur-of-the-moment encounters more valuable. You never know what might come from deciding to strike up a conversation with someone as you walk in from the parking lot, or when you invite a new employee to lunch. Remember to risk reaching out.

Some companies actively set up opportunities for ChoicePoints for employees, knowing that casual conversations often lead to new ideas and projects. An April 2013 *New York Times* article, "Engineering Serendipity," tells about researchers at Arizona State University, who asked people to wear "sociometric badges" that measured all sorts of things: movements, speech, patterns of conversation. "Participants felt most creative on days spent in motion meeting people, not working for long stretches at their desks," said Ben Waber, a visiting scientist at Massachusetts Institute of Technology and cofounder of the company that makes the badges. "Employees who ate at cafeteria tables designed for 12 were more productive than those at tables for four, thanks to more chance conversations and larger social networks." Waber's studies show that productivity rises when the number of people you meet during the workday increases. Combine more chance meetings with honed relationship-building skills and the results will show up, not only in higher productivity, but also in increased engagement, collaboration, and innovation.

Prepping for ChoicePoints

"Yesterday I got to work early, and as I waited for the elevator, I was completely preoccupied with thoughts of the meeting I was going to lead in a few minutes. Just as the elevator doors closed, I realized that someone had stepped in behind me. I turned around, and to my surprise it was none other than Charles Bolden, our new administrator at NASA.

"That's right, the top guy at my agency. Newly appointed by President Obama. Sure wish I'd been ready for *that* conversation. So, what did I say as we rode up together? I have no idea! I can tell you what I *wished* I'd said, because I've played it over and over in my mind. I *wish* I'd welcomed him and congratulated him on his incredible career as an astronaut. I *wish* I'd asked him how his first three days at NASA had been. I *wish* I'd told him about the great work my team had done renegotiating a new agreement with one of our international partners.

"But to tell you the truth . . . I have no idea. The elevator ride and the conversation—it's all a total blur. I'm kicking myself, because I was so unprepared. That silent ride was my wake-up call."

You can create more ChoicePoints in your life by noticing the possibilities in the areas listed below.

Hobby/Health/Sports Activities. Some of Pat's first customers, when he started his home-based graphic design business, were the people he'd met singing in a barbershop quartet. As you enjoy leisure-time activities, remember to teach others about your skills and talents and listen with an ear for how you can contribute to the quality of their personal and professional lives. Listen also for resources and ideas you can take back into your workplace.

Sondra and Marilyn both showed up at the health club at 6 A.M. on Mondays, Wednesdays, and Fridays. They could have just continued to exchange pleasantries, but instead used their exercise time to develop a relationship through which they supported each other's journey as new managers. Even though they worked in very different companies, they shared many of the same people challenges. Two years and lots of miles on the treadmill later, they knew that the confidential support and advice they'd given each other had been crucial to their professional growth and success.

Kid Connections. Your son plays on a soccer team or takes swimming lessons. How many times have you waited impatiently for the coach to end practice when you could have been developing your relationships with other parents?

Kudos to Amy whose sidelines conversations with Jackie resulted in Amy providing management training for Jackie's organization—even though their daughters were on rival teams!

Seatmates. There you are in the airplane for three hours, elbow to elbow with a fellow traveler. Sure you might want to read or nap, but remember that a lot of people build business relationships with people they meet on airplanes.

On a trip to New York, Bob sat next to David, a sales rep for a box manufacturing company. Bob told David he was looking for a heart-shaped box for his company's new specialty food product. David sent him the specs the next day and got the contract.

Wild Cards. Seeking out ways to network with people whose views, interests, and backgrounds are completely different from yours broadens your horizon in unexpected ways. As you make contact with people outside your regular circles, each conversation becomes an adventure. Assume that everyone you meet is important. These wild card contacts can be winners. Anywhere people are is a networking opportunity . . . if you have the know-how.

Alan Cole, a strategy consultant in Washington, D.C., told us, "People like who they know, but they don't know who they like." He was referring to people's propensity to seek out people like themselves. He says it's like a default setting: "Deep in the system is a setting you forgot you clicked on long ago, and now it rules you and limits who you reach out to." Seeking out Wild Cards is a way to open yourself to new experiences. "First you make your choices, then your choices make you," Cole says.

ChoicePoints are, by definition, one-on-one encounters that arise out of proximity. But you can also *intentionally* put yourself in situations where you meet more people.

Connect in Groups

By joining groups, you more closely target the kinds of people you want to meet and develop relationships with. For any given job type, industry, business, or interest, you'll have many possible groups to choose from.

Jon is a partner in a mid-sized architectural firm in Baltimore, Maryland. He specializes in designing hospitals and has a personal and professional interest in landscaping. He could join the American Institute of Architects, and any of its many special interest groups. He could join the Board of Trade, and the American Institute of Landscape Architects, and the local Rotary Club. He could join the American Association of Hospital Administrators, and the Chesapeake Healthcare Association. Then there's the group that's restoring plant life along the Chesapeake Bay. Or how about the Lion's Club? Or he could join the alumni group for his alma mater, Boston University. Or how about a referral group? Jon has many possibilities. You do too. Jon needs a process to narrow down the choices and find the best groups for him. So do you.

CHOOSE GROUPS STRATEGICALLY

Use the list that follows as you make strategic choices about groups to become involved with outside your organization. These groups have membership rosters, leaders, and regular meetings. To reap the benefits, you'll need to do more than attend; you'll need to participate. Don't be a knee-jerk joiner, taking the first thing that comes along or making the easiest choice. Not all groups are equally useful for networking. Your choice will depend on your goals and on the characteristics of the group.

Not all networking groups are equally useful.

The possibilities below are arranged from the most highly structured and intentional groups at the top of the list, to the least network-focused groups at the bottom. The groups at the top focus on bringing people together to do business; the groups farther down the list have other goals and networking becomes a sideline. Groups at the top will actually teach you how to network and outline appropriate behaviors. In groups farther down the list, the ground rules are foggier, so the more skilled at networking you are, the more successful you'll be.

As you read down the list below, think about which groups would fit your purposes best.

Customer Common Groups. These groups are made up of businesses that have customers in common. For instance, professionals who support people though all kinds of business and life transitions, such as a CPA, an estate attorney, a real estate agent, and a business consultant, might band together to refer work to each other. These groups are usually created by the members themselves. If your goal is business development, you may want to start a group like this.

Special Purpose Networks. Some networks are created with one purpose in mind. In Chicago, for example, entrepreneurs started a special network to attract venture financing. Another example is a group of 12 editors, who all work for alumni magazines at large universities, and who talk online and meet face to face twice a year to share resources, ideas, and support. Some of these special purpose networks are formed by members themselves; others rise out of associations and industry organizations.

Business Referral Groups. Small- or home-based businesspeople, sales professionals, or people in professional services benefit most from these groups. A referral group's mission is tightly focused on getting business and generating referrals for and from each other. Only one business in each professional category may join. For example, the group might include one banker, one lawyer, one accountant, etc. At meetings, members learn about each other's services. A commitment to attend and generate leads is essential to the success of the group.

Networking Organizations. These groups often have the word "networking" in their names. They may have other goals, too, such as professional development for members, but their main goal is to provide relationship-building opportunities. To help people get acquainted, these organizations may offer special interest subgroups, such as for people doing business internationally or for recent college graduates. One women's networking organization in Kansas City had as its motto: "The thing that sets us apart is the people we bring together."

Professional and Trade Associations. Whatever your job type, whatever your industry or profession, there is a professional association for you—probably several. Ask experienced people in your chosen field to recommend which one—or ones—would be right for you. Watch the business section of your newspaper for meeting announcements. Check the Encyclopedia of Associations, or go to the appropriate professional group's website for membership information and to find the chapter nearest you. The goals are professional development, networking for career and business resources, and sometimes lobbying.

Industry-Specific Organizations. These organizations put you in touch with people in other companies in your industry. An aviation association, for example, brings together people from all of the carriers, as well as related businesses. Because they face similar problems, these people can be great resources for each other. Participation in one of these groups could lead to upward mobility, since there is usually a lot of opportunity for job movement between similar organizations. Becoming active could also give you access to all kinds of state-of-the-art resources, best practices, novel ideas, and information to help you do your job and to improve your overall organization. Within these industry-specific groups, there often are subgroups for people with various kinds of jobs—a purchasing group, for example. These subgroups give you an entrée to your peers and leaders across the industry.

Chambers of Commerce. Whether you're self-employed or work for an organization, the Chamber will welcome you. Although this group's mission focuses on civic improvement, economic development, and legislative initiatives that favor business, at Chamber meetings you'll come in contact with people from a wide variety of workplaces with a wide variety of interests. Networking is certainly a big part of the picture.

Civic and Service Organizations. These groups include such organizations as Rotary International, the Lions Club, and many others. They focus on service to the community and civic improvement. In a relaxed, informal atmosphere, you'll have conversations that help others trust you and, long term, can lead to job opportunities, new customers, and access to all kinds of resources.

Volunteer Groups. Volunteering is a way to blend a passion for giving back to the community with the chance to learn new skills and establish long term business relationships. When Simon agreed to help build new play equipment for the community park, little did he know setting up the swings with Martin would lead to a contract for his company to videotape corporate presentations at Martin's company for the next five years.

Alumni Groups. A special kind of camaraderie grows out of having attended the same school. Alumni clubs put you in touch with people of all ages and walks of life. Although these clubs focus on promoting the school, raising funds, or supporting the teams, networking for business benefit is also an important part of the mix.

Religious Organizations. While business may not be the first thing you talk about at your house of worship, it's undeniably true that being active in a religious community does establish relationships from which businesses and careers may eventually grow. Bob and George got to know each other so well at choir practice, that when George was asked to open up a new division for his company in Paris, Bob introduced him to his brother Michael, who'd lived there for 20 years; Michael helped George find an apartment and make new friends.

What's impressive about this list is the variety of groups you can join. To find the right networking groups, associations, or organizations for you, check the Internet, the phone book, your local library, or the business pages of your newspaper. Ask other people in your profession what organizations they benefit from the most. Ask customers and clients what groups they belong to. There may be an "associate member" category if you are a supplier or vendor.

EXPLORE IN-HOUSE GROUPS

Some groups are inside your organization, like the Hispanic Employee Resource Group or a community of practice. Even if you work from home or work at an office far away from others on your team, you can still benefit from belonging to some groups in your organization. The people you meet will learn what kinds of things to come to you for, what kind of projects to collaborate with you on. You'll hear about big initiatives and new trends.

Roberta was a new hire at a large insurance company. She figured that a good way to better understand her job would be to learn more about the big picture. She joined the Women's Innovation Network (WIN). "It gives me a sense of purpose outside my day-to-day work. WIN makes a big promise," Roberta says, "but it really comes through. The website says, 'Knowledge tends to remain hidden until it is asked for and shared.' That's why WIN exists—it's an exchange of ideas and a web of relationships." After just a year of participating, Roberta knows she's gotten good tips about advancing her career, and she's found people to collaborate on some enterprise-wide projects.

CHECK IT OUT BEFORE YOU JOIN

Once you've identified a few groups, remember that you are about to place a very talented person—you—in a key position, so look before you leap. Attend a couple of meetings as a guest. Talk to new members and board members. Read several issues of the newsletter. Scan the membership directory. Before you hand over your—or your organization's—money and commit your time, assess the group's potential value to you by answering these questions:

1. How many members are there? (In general, the bigger the better for networking, but it may be easier to move into leadership positions or gain visibility in other ways when you join a smaller group.)

2. Can I get excited about the group's mission? Will its activities help me reach my networking goals? Are people in the group likely to provide valuable resources or information?

3. Are people in the group likely to need my product or service or to refer business to me? What do people say about the group? What's its reputation in the profession or community?

4. What opportunities will the group offer me to associate with my peers? With the well-known gurus in the field?

5. Does the group set a good networking culture by encouraging people to introduce themselves and talk to each other about important business and career challenges?

6. Does the group have special activities to help newcomers feel welcome and meet people?

7. How easy is it to participate? How quickly could I move into a leadership role that would give me visibility, access to best practices, and introductions to people I'd like to know?

8. Do the leaders seem genuinely excited about their participation or are they playing "somebody has to do it?"

9. Are the programs cutting edge? Do the topics and speakers provide valuable professional growth? Will they offer best practices I can take back to my organization?

10. What would my time commitment be? Can I make that commitment for at least one year?

11. What exactly could I contribute to this group in order to become visible?

The 10 Biggest Mistakes Members Make

1. They join, but don't go. They show up so sporadically that they don't reap the many benefits of membership.

2. They appear, but don't interact. They eat another olive, listen to the speaker, and leave.

3. They skip the networking portion, arriving just in time for the meal. They duck out just as the speaker finishes. They talk and sit with people they already know.

4. They make no effort to be visible; instead, they try to blend into the crowd.

5. They wait for others to make the first moves.

6. They think exchanging contact information is networking.

7. They give up too soon. They hop from one organization to another, never giving themselves or others time to establish trusting relationships.

8. They have "non-conversations" about the weather and the ballgame scores. They never get around to talking about things that will build the relationship.

9. They arrive without an Agenda. They come without any idea of what they have to Give or what they want to Get.

10. They are unaware of the rules of "netiquette" within the group. (Each group has them!) They violate the "good networking" protocols of the group.

ORCHESTRATE WHO KNOWS YOU

Joining a group doesn't mean you join anybody's network—or that they join yours. But membership does give you a place where you can develop relationships with your fellow members. Great networkers work on making themselves valuable and as a consequence, memorable. Joining a group helps you expand the number of people you know and the number of people who know you, if you use your participation to:

- Demonstrate your skills and expertise.

- Find new resources and best practices.

- Showcase the products and services you and your organization offer.

- Establish your reputation with people you want to network with.

- Attract new employees and new vendors.

- Discover new career directions or make a job change.

- Gain recognition for your accomplishments and successes.

So take a high-profile role in groups you belong to. Write an article for the newsletter. Provide a program. Be the person who figures out how to attract lots of new members. Get elected to the board of directors. Set up a job bank, if your group doesn't have one. Enter your work in the annual awards program—an excellent way to become known for your abilities. Demonstrate your speaking skills, your budgetary wizardry, your organizing expertise, or your leadership prowess.

When people see you in action in a group, they make up their minds about who you are—even if they've never been personally introduced to you. If you do a great job as treasurer, people will assume that you are also an excellent IT manager or an outstanding sales professional. Conversely, if you've promised to do something, but don't come through, people will assume that you are not a competent attorney or public relations practitioner either. It's the All-or-Nothing Rule: If you do one thing well, people will assume you do everything well. Take heed: If you do one thing poorly, people will assume you do everything poorly.

The strength and expanse of your networks depend on how many people know you so well that when they come across interesting resources or opportunities, you pop into their minds as the person to share them with.

Make the Most of Your Memberships

You probably already are a member of several groups. Knowing what you know about all the possibilities, it's time to assess those groups to see if you are getting what you need from them. Take a look at Mitchell and Mary's memberships.

Mitchell, an immigration lawyer, has two goals: to gain "key player" status in the field of immigration law for himself and his firm, and to attract new clients. Figure 2–1 highlights his involvement in five organizations.

ORGANIZATION	ROLE	BENEFIT	GOALS
George Washington University Alumni Association	Member (attend occasionally)	Service to alma mater; see people from all walks of life	Meet potential clients
Greater Washington Board of Trade	Vice President	Wide visibility (1200 member companies)	Collaborate with and get referrals from CPA firms; meet potential clients
Maryland Bar Association	Member	Professional development	Professional development; referrals

(continues)

| Casa de Maryland | Committee Chair; occasional speaker | Develop leadership skills; partner with other firms | Get new clients; look for new hires |
| American Immigration Lawyers Association | Member; on local program committee | Professional development | Get referrals; expand my ProNet |

FIGURE 2-1. *Mitchell's Memberships*

Mary is a quality assurance supervisor in a health care corporation. She's also a certified management coach and active in accreditation programs. Figure 2–2 highlights her involvement in five organizations.

ORGANIZATION	ROLE	BENEFIT	GOALS
American Society for Quality	Member; attend annual conference	Professional development	Stay current in my field
Denver Section, ASQ	Chair	Professional development	Gain leadership and speaking skills
International Coaching Federation	Member, local chapter	Improve coaching skills	Be a part-time coach after retirement in 12 years
Healthcare Quality Association	Member, Chair of Accreditation Committee	Working with people from other companies	Expand my ProNet and learn from others
United Way Campaign	Annual Co-Chair	Develop my OrgNet	Contribute to my community

FIGURE 2-2. *Mary's Memberships*

ASSESS YOUR BENEFITS

Create a similar chart of your memberships, making notes about the nature of your participation. Then itemize the benefits of belonging to each organization. Are you getting what you want from these organizations? If not, are they the wrong ones for you? Or do you need to find more strategic ways to participate? Does being involved contribute to your goals or have you outgrown your need for and interest in the group? Don't start joining new groups if you haven't taken advantage of the opportunities in groups you're already a part of. Another question that will help you assess your participation is, "Where have I developed the most profitable contacts in the past?"

As Mitchell looked over his involvements in Figure 2–1, he decided that although Alumni Association events were fun, he'd be more likely to find new clients elsewhere. He noticed that his reasons for joining the Board of Trade were working out well. Several new clients in recent months had come from his activity in that group. He felt the Bar Association was still a must. He decided to continue his involvement with Casa de Maryland, realizing that the community service was very satisfying, even though he hadn't even thought of that as a goal. Reviewing his membership in the American Immigration Lawyers Association, he realized that he was spending too much time on the program committee and that he'd rather get involved at the national and international level, since his firm now had offices in San Francisco and Mexico City. Probably the biggest outcome for Mitchell was that he decided to start a monthly check-in process with his colleagues at work, so they could work together to deploy people to many different networking groups. As the firm grew, he could see the value in being known and visible in many different organizations.

Decide if networking groups are paying off.

Look back at Figure 2–2. When Mary took stock of how the groups she was in served her purposes, she decided to postpone her involvement in the International Coaching Federation until she got closer to her retirement date. And since she had cochaired the United Way campaign at her company for the last four years, she decided to bow out of that in favor of getting active in a couple of the Employee Resource Groups that had interesting programs and would help her get more of a big-picture view of the rapidly expanding organization she worked for.

Over time, you'll find that you outgrow organizations or that a group just isn't paying off for you the way you'd hoped. You may discover that you haven't been as active as you should have been to reap the benefits you desire. This kind of evaluation is part of being strategic about your networking. Make it an annual event to assess what your memberships are doing for you.

Choose Your Goal

You are CEO, president, and chairman of the board of your networks. So customize them to fit your needs. They won't be duplicates of anybody else's networks. They will include a unique set of contacts developed for your unique set of reasons. Your goal determines the scope of your networking project.

If your networking goal is small, it might require only a small networking project—one that can be accomplished in less than six months and is made up of only a couple of activities. It will require only a limited number of networking contacts (a KeyNet; see Chapter 4 for a full discussion) and a limited amount of money, time, and effort. Wanting to benchmark your department's processes and procedures, for example, you might put together a group of several people in your professional association who have similar jobs. As each person hosts one meeting and provides an overview of his department, you'll all get a better idea of how your workplaces measure up.

If your goal is medium-sized, it might require a larger networking project—one that could take six months to a year, with a corresponding outlay of money, time, and effort. Say you want to fulfill your department's new objective: "Raise the visibility of our bank with small business owners." You could create a networking project that includes a variety of substantial activities. You might join the Chamber and immediately volunteer for a committee that plans Chamber programs for small businesses. And you might put together—and get bank sponsorship for—a workshop for members of the Home-Based Business Association. Over time, you'll be able to open up many opportunities to meet small businesses owners.

If your goal is very far-reaching, you'll need to create a large-scale networking effort—one that might take several years and require commitment, perhaps even self-sacrifice, not to mention money, time, and effort. These big, long-term, life-changing efforts are what we call "Strategic Positioning Projects" (SPPs for short). They include many kinds of networking activities, pursued with high commitment. They will position you to be the natural and only choice when opportunity knocks.

PLAN YOUR STRATEGIC POSITIONING PROJECT

Here's how to get started planning your big project to reach your big goal. There are many kinds of networking activities you can select from as you pursue your SPP. You can even put together a group to help you brainstorm what they might be. Or glean ideas from stories in the business press, such as the *Wall Street Journal* or *Fast Company*. Or ask colleagues or mentors for ideas. Or borrow models and adapt ideas from what others have done. You'll find dozens of ideas throughout this book.

* *

Design a large-scale, long-term networking project.

* *

Use your contacts within your organization, your community, your profession, or your industry to do some preliminary research about possible activities. Then, outline your networking options. Projects evolve. You'll constantly be tweaking your SPP as the months go by. When we interviewed hundreds of networkers, we noticed that their SPPs had similar characteristics. Most of their big-time, long-term, networking efforts could pass at least four out of the five tests discussed below.

1. *The Doorway Test.* To pass the Doorway Test, ask yourself, "Who do I need to know? Who are my ideal customers, clients, or employers? Where will I find these people? Where do they spend time? How can I go where they go and become visible to them?"

Ideally your SPP will position you so that the people who can help you achieve your goal will just stream by. Find—or create—a "doorway." Put yourself in that doorway, so you meet the right people and they begin to know you and trust you.

Find or create the "doorway" that the right people pass through.

Melinda, a partner in a CPA firm, didn't have to look far to find the "doorway" that would lead to her goal: a constant stream of women business owners as clients. She asked a longtime client to propose her name for the board of directors of the Women's Business Center, whose mission is to guide and support women business owners. The board position gave her credibility and visibility. Melinda also taught classes at the Center on financial matters for growing businesses— whether they were start-ups or pulling in revenues of a million or more. As woman business owners became familiar with Melinda's expertise, quite a few selected her as their CPA.

To pass the Doorway Test, figure out where you'll meet the people you want to meet and make yourself so central that they can't help but notice you.

2. *The All-or-Nothing Test.* This test expands on the ideas in the All-or-Nothing Rule we mentioned earlier: If people see you doing one thing well, they will assume that you are good at everything; if people see you doing one thing poorly, they will assume that you do nothing well. Ask yourself: "Is my SPP a vehicle for demonstrating my value and abilities? Even if my networking activity has nothing to do with my exact area of career expertise, when I'm involved in this activity, will people just naturally make the leap that I must be good at my work?"

Evan wanted to become known to government human resources professionals who could hire the trainers and consultants his firm placed. Over many years, he became active in the Training Officers Conference, a professional group that meets monthly and has an annual conference. He showcased his approach to training and development in a luncheon speech he gave for the group. He became known to others by working on the Awards Committee. He soaked up information on trends and challenges from the many professional development programs he attended and from the conversations he had with contacts. He looked for ways to support other members and funnel good information to them. His long-term commitment to the well-being of the group and the people he met there made many in the group think of his firm first when they needed training and consulting services.

Do one thing well and get a reputation for doing everything well.

To pass the All-or-Nothing Test, be sure your SPP gives you a way to showcase your abilities. Then, perform brilliantly. That way, you'll get a reputation for doing everything well.

3. *The Bottom-Line Test.* To pass this test, ask yourself, "Can I arrange the time in my schedule and do I have the money in my budget to support my SPP? Will my networking efforts take me one step closer to my goal?"

Louisa is a financial planner whose long-term goal is to be invited to give a daily two-minute financial tip for women on CNN. To prepare for that opportunity, she found a networking contact to propose her as host for a monthly show for women on her local cable TV station. She's developed a circle of contacts at the station and is learning from them everything she'll need to know. Louisa estimates that her SPP will cost her about $5,000 this year and take about two days a month. That's a substantial investment, but she's confident that the experience she's gaining with her show will lead to a syndicated show and ultimately that call from CNN.

To pass the Bottom-Line Test, make sure you are spending your time and money in the best way to reach your goal. Put together an SPP with a big impact.

4. *The Five-Year Test.* To pass this test, ask yourself, "Does my SPP set the stage for the very special phone call I want to receive in three to five years?"

Jon, a director in finance, was looking for a way to make a bigger contribution to his organization and to prepare himself for promotion. Nothing surprising about those goals. But his SPP took a unique approach. He knew that his CFO was increasingly concerned that their company wasn't on the cutting edge of using technology to make decisions critical to the business. Jon decided to get ready for a job that didn't even appear yet on his company's organization chart— "techno-finance chief." He started making his plan in 2009 after reading a survey from his professional association that outlined new technologies that could impact the role of finance in organizations.

With his CFO's support, Jon began to build his expertise through attendance at conferences and in other ways. He focused on business analytics, using data to predict, not just to report. He built strong ties with the IT department and collaborated with several individuals on purchasing software. He used the resources of his professional association repeatedly, interviewing people in other companies, and participating in a focus group with his peers. In 2014, he got the call. He was promoted to VP-finance/technology. His boss had been his strong advocate throughout this long process and acknowledged that

Jon's growing expertise and innovative work had benefitted the corporation in many ways.

To pass the Five-Year Test, be sure every activity in your SPP helps to create that all-important phone call down the road.

. . . .

Your project will make you the natural and only choice.

. . . .

5. *The Pig-in-Mud Test.* Ask yourself, "Does my SPP represent a magnificent blend of my unique personal and professional interests and passions? Does it represent who I am, what I value, what I like to do, where I want to go, and what I do best? Will my SPP make me 'as happy as a pig in mud'?" If you have seen pigs in mud, you know what we mean. They wallow. They roll. They close their eyes in ecstasy. They are happy, content, comfortable, and want to be right where they are and nowhere else.

Morris, owner of a mortgage company, graduated from a university 15 years ago. An active alum and avid supporter of the university's basketball team, he had a strong network of contacts in the Alumni Association. He created an SPP that helped his alma mater, gave him a way to expand his business in a very natural way, and made him very happy. Here's how it happened. It came to his attention that the president of the university didn't have any discretionary funds to use for worthy projects that came up from time to time. So Morris offered to start a fund called the President's Club. Through networking, Morris assembled a group of generous donors who created a fund for the president to use on innovative projects that would improve the university's visibility and attract talented students. When students wanted to enter a robotics contest in Japan, the president offered to buy their supplies and their airline tickets with money from the fund. Imagine how the president bragged about his students when they won the contest! Imagine how grateful he was to Morris for creating the fund! In his fund-raising campaign, Morris found that alums often asked about his business and some wanted him to handle their mortgages. Morris expanded his business, so that he could do mortgages in many states and took his business to a whole new level. To pass the Pig-in-Mud Test, be sure your SPP makes you happy in life and at work!

In case you thought that great connections "just happen," or that "some people are just in the right place at the right time," we hope you're now convinced that being deliberate and intentional is the way to get results. As Alvin Toffler, futurist and former associate editor of *Fortune Magazine* once said, "You've got to think about big things while you're doing small things, so that all the small things go in the right direction."

Notice that, in the Network-Oriented Workplace, your job has become Job + N(etworking) with three strategic focuses—getting your work done, getting to contribute to organization-wide goals, and getting ahead. You network casually at ChoicePoints, and in groups, both inside and outside your organization. You plan for these interactions by making Agendas, and you bring all your networking and planning skills to bear as you use networking to reach your big goals through Strategic Positioning Projects.

3

....

Envision Your
Ideal Network

Strategic Connections: Link Up HR Leaders

At a large defense contractor, the corporate-level human resources executives envisioned a larger, more proactive role for HR professionals. They selected 16 up-and-coming HR managers from the four business units for a two-year leadership program. One executive said, "Serving more than 100,000 employees across the enterprise, these people need new ways to connect and collaborate to deal with new challenges. There's no way to train people for the future, but if they build relationships across business boundaries, they'll be able to create the synergy to cope with ever-changing issues."

BUILDING NETWORKING relationships across internal boundaries and even outside the perimeters creates the strong ties the Network-Oriented Workplace needs. Competency 3 is all about how to increase the scope and balance of your network.

The Four Nets

ur Nets: a WorkNet, an OrgNet, a ProNet, and a
er these terms describe your ideal network. Take a
–1, The Four Nets Matrix.

To be a success and achieve your greatest potential, you'll make and maintain relationships in all Four Nets and leverage contacts, resources, and information from one Net to another.

What's the purpose of thinking in terms of "Nets"? You may be like Nick, who said, "I know a lot of people. I just don't know what to do with them." Nets help you to see clearly what kinds of contacts you have and where the holes are. Nets help you take a strategic look at

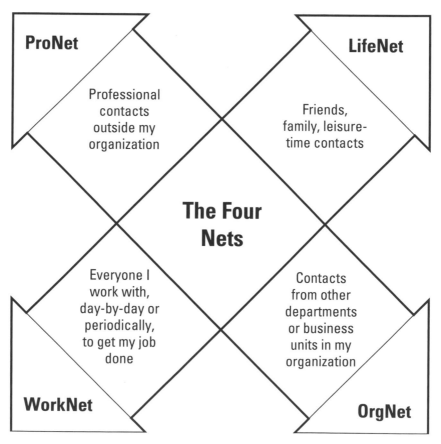

FIGURE 3-1. *The Four Nets Matrix*

your contacts—their commonalities, their professional expertise, their diversity, and their range. As you think about who you know in each of your Four Nets, you'll probably notice that you have some underdeveloped areas. As you add contacts, you will expand and strengthen your networks.

. . . .

Nets help you take a strategic look at your contacts.

. . . .

YOUR WORKNET

Your WorkNet includes everyone you work with day-by-day or periodically to get your job done. It includes current coworkers, team members, clients/customers, partners, vendors/suppliers, consultants, contractors, and people you work with remotely. WorkNet contacts are, for the most part, assigned, not chosen by you. They're a given. But establishing productive and collaborative relationships with these people doesn't happen automatically.

Nancy's WorkNet includes the six people she supervises, two contractors, and her boss. One supervisee is in Rome. Her boss is 200 miles away in New York City. Another very important person in her WorkNet is the budget officer, Sam, with whom she works closely for several days each quarter. Notice that people in your WorkNet don't necessarily work in your department and may not even be employees at all.

Alejandro, in finance, works with Tim, Maria, and Swansetta almost every day. He only works with Patty when they are preparing numbers for the annual report, but they stay in touch all year long. When annual report time comes along, they're ready to collaborate.

WorkNet contacts help you:

1. Get the job done.

2. Be more productive.

3. Unsnarl bureaucratic tie-ups.

4. Round up or draw on talent.

5. Access inside information.

6. Find resources.

7. Solve problems.

8. Make better decisions and "field-test" ideas.

WorkNet challenges include:

- Balancing relationship-building activities with your task responsibilities.

- Knowing how to start and cultivate relationships.

- Getting relationships back on track if friction occurs.

- Systematically learning about the skills, expertise, capabilities, and interests of the people you work with, so you can get the job done and draw on the talents of others in your work group to the maximum.

One pitfall in WorkNet relationships is that it's easy to get so busy that you forget to appreciate the people on your team. Sumit said, "I don't have time to constantly say thanks for this and thanks for that. It's their job, for heaven's sake!" Sumit would probably get more done in the long run if he found easy, informal ways to say "Job well-done!" or "Thanks for your help." Write a note, find a relevant cartoon, bring in a snack, think of another way to let someone know that you don't take his or her contributions for granted.

YOUR ORGNET

Unlike your WorkNet, your OrgNet is entirely created by you. It's made up of people in other divisions, departments, and business units of the organization. Jim in HR met Chris in IT when they both took a three-day training program at the company's headquarters. They found they had much in common and much to learn from each other. They make it a point to have lunch every month or so to compare notes on company strategy and look for areas where their initiatives or expertise could help each other. Your OrgNet gives you a way to stay in touch with enterprise-wide contacts up and down the hierarchy. Because your OrgNet spans internal barriers and reaches out to include people at various levels, it exemplifies the Network-Oriented Workplace. The OrgNet you create is far more complex, diverse, and useful than any organization chart.

Your OrgNet leaps boundaries and ignores ranks.

When Nancy started her job as purchasing manager she made it a point to eat lunch in the cafeteria with someone from a different department at least two or three times a week. She asked each of them lots of questions to get to know them and to gain an understanding of their emerging issues and upcoming challenges. Her relationships helped her anticipate needs and know who to call when questions came up.

Your OrgNet contacts may be people you've met as you work on special task forces, go to training programs, or participate in events hosted by communities of practice and employee resource groups. They may be mentors and other key contacts, but are not in your immediate work group.

OrgNet contacts help you:

1. See ways to contribute on a large scale, have an impact, create change.

2. Bolster the bottom line.

3. Support organizational initiatives.

4. Act like a leader, not just an employee.

5. Create a safety net in case there are layoffs.

6. Stay tuned into the big picture.

7. Find new career opportunities.

8. Make your skills visible to a wider group of people.

OrgNet challenges include:

- Being strategic, efficient, and skillful in reaching out and staying in touch.

- Assessing the cultural ground rules. As your networker identity develops, you will find reaching out beyond your job responsibilities easier. Your new skills will help you feel more comfortable as you risk reaching out. If you feel your organization hasn't yet overtly acknowledged the value of your networking activities and encouraged them, ask people in your OrgNet if they feel they not only have permission to network, but are being asked to do so. You probably will find that any concerns you've had will disappear.

- Noticing and creating opportunities to connect with people outside your WorkNet.

- Finding appropriate ways to initiate contact with people above you in the hierarchy.

One pitfall in creating your OrgNet is that you may feel too busy to relate to any more people. At the beginning of one of our training programs Sam said loud and clear, "I really don't have time to develop an OrgNet. Besides, everybody else is as busy as I am—they don't want to hear from me!" By the end of the two-day workshop, he'd found so much value in connecting with people in the class—all of whom were outside of his department—that he was singing a different tune. He eagerly made plans to get together with André, Maria, and Randy in the coming weeks and volunteered to spearhead a cross-functional group to look at ways to consolidate the number of vendor relationships the company had.

Choosing to Be Visible

"We'd been without a manager for four months, and I missed having someone to bounce ideas off of, someone to encourage me, someone I could learn from. Then we got the announcement. Jan, from another division, was going to transfer over to lead our team. We were excited—we'd heard she was an excellent boss, and had heard her speak at several all-hands meetings. She'd been with the company just about as long as I had—14 years.

"In our first one-on-one meeting, she said she'd looked over my work, and she congratulated me on a couple of recent projects. Then she said, 'I wonder why I haven't heard of you.'

"That statement really made me stop and think. Why was I invisible? Here I was working away, yet nobody except my five teammates knew anything about what I could do. This bothered me. How would people ever know what kinds of things to involve me in if nobody knew what I was good at?

"When I learned about the Four Nets, I realized my OrgNet was nonexistent. Not only do I want people to know my capabilities, but also I wonder what greater visibility could lead to down the road."

YOUR PRONET

Your ProNet consists of professional contacts outside the organization. It includes people you know through your membership in professional associations or service clubs, people you used to work with in previous jobs, former clients/customers, partners, vendors/suppliers, consultants, contractors, and virtual workers, along with other contacts you've chosen to build relationships with for professional reasons.

Some of them may be professional connections you've made on LinkedIn or similar sites. Omar worked with Jared at a previous job, and now they enjoy sharing best practices and noticing trends in their profession—mostly through Internet conversations. Lee also learns from peers in other organizations, people he sees regularly at his local professional association meetings. He's on the program committee because taking an active role lets him showcase his skills and become known to others. Omar and Lee both look for opportunities to take good ideas from their ProNets back into their own organizations.

Seth, a technical editor, is a member of the International Association of Business Communicators. When he was looking for a job in corporate communications, it didn't take him long to find someone in IABC who was leaving her job to go back to graduate school and who knew his talents because of their work together on a committee. She was eager to refer him for the job.

ProNet contacts help you:

1. Develop professionally and increase your mastery and expertise, so you can get your job done and contribute ideas to your larger organization.

2. Benchmark your skills and stay market-ready.

3. Provide valuable BringBack—tips, trends, business intelligence, best practices to share with your colleagues.

4. Find career advancement opportunities.

5. Give back to your profession as you teach and mentor others.

ProNet challenges include:

- Making strategic decisions about what groups to join.

- Spending your time and money wisely.

- Becoming visible and showing who you are and what you're good at in everything you do and say.

- Making the effort to start and maintain relationships.

- Introducing new ideas and ways of doing things into your organization.

- Finding the time and money to participate.

One pitfall in developing and using your ProNet is the time it takes. Daichi explained why he was reluctant to reach out when he had a question or a challenge, even when he thought others in his professional circle might have answers. "It's probably not worth the time to ask people for help. It's usually just easier to figure it out by myself rather than get other people involved. And besides, I don't want to owe too many favors."

As Daichi develops his networker identity, he'll realize that two heads really are better than one. Giving James or Nancy a quick call will get him information faster and perhaps a new perspective or insight. Asking for help also builds relationships by solidifying trust. After all, would you ask someone you *didn't* trust?

YOUR LIFENET

Your LifeNet is made up of family, friends, and leisure-time contacts. It includes people who share your interests, people in non–work-oriented organizations, such as your alumni association or your place of worship. It includes neighbors, people you meet socially or when you exercise, and fellow volunteers.

You may stay up to date with many of them on Facebook, as well as getting together face to face. They bring you a wealth of information, support, and resources. Even though you meet these people in the personal realm of your life, they can have a tremendous impact on your career.

John's LifeNet has enriched his work life. John finds Frank, his next-door neighbor, a great sounding board for workplace concerns. When Frank's college-age daughter was looking for a summer internship, John introduced her to the right people in his company. John also learns a lot from his sister-in-law. She's an experienced manager in a different company and industry, so having been in a similar role for just six months, he asks for confidential advice on tricky situations.

> *Your LifeNet brings you a wealth of information, support, and resources.*

Bob and Juan met each other at an alumni association golf tournament. Both engineers, their friendship flourished. Several years later they decided to start their own engineering consulting firm.

LifeNet contacts help you:

1. Feel the joy and camaraderie of going through life in community.

2. Gain access to diverse kinds of information and resources.

3. Celebrate when times are good and commiserate when times are bad.

4. Develop new skills in a nonthreatening environment.

5. Meet new contacts whose skills or resources may be useful at work.

LifeNet challenges include:

• Reinventing your LifeNet as you go through the stages of life, for instance, when you move, or work abroad, or face an empty nest, or experience changes in your marital status, or develop new interests, or retire.

- Staying in touch with people when work demands are high.

- Realizing that many things you share with friends and family (especially electronically!) might not be appropriate for people in your other three Nets to know—unfortunately, everything that happens on Facebook stays on Facebook.

One common pitfall you might face in developing a strong LifeNet is the temptation to "quarantine" your personal relationships. Bob, a financial planner, said, "I like to keep business and personal separate. And besides, my mother-in-law would never understand what I do." Lloyd, a CPA, said, "Sure I get together with the guys to play basketball every week, but we don't talk about *work*." Too bad! Learning how to bring resources, ideas, and people from one Net to another is one thing that truly savvy networkers do with ease—to the great advantage of everyone involved. Your networks thrive when you bring in out-of-the ordinary information and out-of-the box solutions.

To sum up:

- Your WorkNet helps you get the job done.

- Your OrgNet helps you stay in touch with the big picture and contribute to the overall success of your organization.

- Your ProNet helps you gain expertise and mastery in your chosen profession, keeps you in touch with larger business trends, and provides opportunities to give back to your profession.

- Your LifeNet helps you create community, get the most out of life, and connect to—and contribute to—abundance for yourself and others.

Looking back at Figure 3–1, The Four Nets Matrix, notice that your WorkNet and OrgNet contacts are all inside your organization. Your ProNet and LifeNet contacts are all outside your organization.

If you take a new job in a new company or change professions, you'll need to develop new contacts in your ProNet to support your new job and function. If you change jobs within your organization, you'll still have access to the same OrgNet, but who you need to know might shift a bit. And since the people in your LifeNet are literally going through life with you, they are considered more long term than short term. But even LifeNet cohorts can and do change over time. When Mary broke her leg skiing she lost touch with some of the folks she met on the slopes, but developed a new set of friends in her rehab at the swimming pool.

The value is in the way your Nets work together. It's about balance and synergy. You'll find that as you leverage contacts and opportunities from one Net to another, you'll have more resources and support at your fingertips and multiply your impact in every area of your life.

Expanding My OrgNet

"My director called me and said, 'How about representing us on a corporate cross-sector team to figure out skill sets we'll want new hires to have in the future. You'll be good at this.'

"I was already super busy, but I figured the chance to work with people I didn't know from all five different sectors of the company was too good to pass up, so I agreed. We met virtually several times using the company's intranet. As the deadline for the report approached we all agreed there would be value in a face-to-face meeting to finish the project. I think the virtual teleconference method becomes less and less effective as you get into the subtleties of a project like this. We set up a two-day offsite where we could all meet, leverage the best talents in the group, and complete the project. Because the face-to-face meeting sped up the information sharing and trust-building, we finished on time and even received a corporate award to acknowledge our accomplishments.

"The hidden, long-term benefit of doing this project was that each of us now had a new network across the corporation. When any of us have questions or concerns about our work, we get in touch with one another to ask for advice. This, in my opinion, is just as valuable to the company as the actual project we finished."

Developing Your Nets

To assess the state of your Nets, list five or more prime contacts in each Net. As you come up with names, you may notice that you've neglected to cultivate contacts in one or two of your Nets. Ask yourself, "Where are the holes? What kinds of contacts am I missing?" Sometimes life gets in the way of network building. For instance, Jake was the single father of two children under five and also cared for his elderly father who lived nearby. Understandably, he had neglected his ProNet. As soon as his LifeNet stopped needing so much of his attention, he rejoined his professional association and revved up his ProNet. On the other hand, Helen realized she'd neglected her LifeNet because her job was so demanding. She started scheduling more time with friends and immediately felt less stressed.

Do you have contacts in all Four Nets?

Take a look at four people with four very different Net-balance challenges.

George's WorkNet was ailing. George was a results-oriented, hard-driving taskmaster. When several people he managed got burnt out and left his team, he decided that one way to boost morale would be to make it a point to celebrate and appreciate more of the milestones and achievements of people in his WorkNet. Every Friday afternoon, he asked himself, "Who do I appreciate this week?" He found unique and fun ways to acknowledge individuals, as well as the group. He gave baseball tickets to Ken. He sent a funny "Congrats on a job well done" card to Jo's home, so her whole family would see it. After a big project was finished, he invited a professional masseuse from his LifeNet to give 10-minute neck massages to anyone who wanted one during the lunch hour. George's WorkNet relationships improved. His team felt more satisfied with the fun and recognition George had introduced.

Marylou's OrgNet needed some nourishment. Marylou noticed that her OrgNet included only people on the second and third floors of the company's headquarters. She wondered, "How can I get to know people on the fourth and fifth floors?" They had a separate cafeteria, so she decided to occasionally eat lunch on the fifth floor. She turned proximity and casual conversations into dynamic and useful relationships. Expanding her OrgNet made all the difference in her understanding of the big picture, her ability to work cross-functionally, and her skill in anticipating needs and solving inter-generational misunderstandings—all assets as she operates in the Network-Oriented Workplace.

> *Your ProNet is your lifeline to new ideas,*
> *best practices, and hot trends.*

Perry's ProNet was desperate for fresh air. When Perry realized that he could think of only a few people in his ProNet, he understood why he felt "stale" and unengaged. He ramped up his participation in his professional association to reestablish his lifeline to new ideas, best practices, and hot trends. As he began to bring back some of the innovative ideas he was learning from his association peers and mentors, he got his spark back, and his supervisees appreciated what they called "the new Perry."

Annette's LifeNet needed a lift. As Annette listed the people in her Four Nets, she began to wonder why she almost never talked about work with her family and friends. Why had she never thought to explore with her exercise buddies or her choir mates what expertise or connections they might have to help her solve work-related problems and professional challenges? Once she decided to occasionally steer the conversation toward work, she got quite a surprise. She discovered that getting to know the young alto sitting next to her in choir practice was a great way to understand more about how to relate to her two new employees who were fresh out of college.

When you have a mental model of your Four Nets, you can develop and draw upon diverse contacts to get the job done. Your connections and collaborations make the Network-Oriented Workplace work and give you the kind of visibility that leads to career success.

Your KeyNets

A KeyNet is a small group of strategically chosen people who can help you achieve one specific goal. When you set a new goal or begin to work on a new project, that's the perfect time to draw together a new KeyNet to help you accomplish it. Include people from at least three and maybe all four of your Four Nets. Assuming you have a project or goal that's bigger than you alone can accomplish—and most are, you will select people for your various KeyNets because of what they can bring to the effort.

Consulting with a few well-chosen key players can assure the success of any special project, and your KeyNets are the way you collaborate to make things happen. In their *Harvard Business Review* article, "Managing Yourself: A Smarter Way to Network," University of Virginia's Rob Cross and Accenture's Robert Thomas say "effective core networks typically range in size from 12 to 18 people." Suppose you want to transfer to your company's office in Tokyo, or revamp your firm's orientation program, or start a new professional association that will serve your specialized niche, or launch a new webcast series to stay in touch with people at remote worksites. Create a KeyNet!

SELECTING YOUR KEYNET

How do you choose the right people?

1. *Start with a goal.* Write your goal or project at the top of a blank sheet of paper. For instance, "Start a summer internship program for my company."

2. *List people.* Choose people from any of your Four Nets to help you get it done. Ask yourself these questions: Who else has a stake in accomplishing this? Who would benefit? Who has influence or information or resources? Who will I have to "get on board" to make this succeed? Who would I enjoy working with? Who can act as a champion?

3. *Look for "connection gaps."* Is it important to have someone from each of your Nets? Ask yourself these questions: Who else will I need to start working with or build a relationship with to achieve my goal? Is this KeyNet diverse with regard to geography, gender, professional role, experience, and age? Who could stop me or significantly slow me down if I don't engage with them? Are there people in my OrgNet I should align with? Have I forgotten any valuable players in my ProNet and LifeNet? Who can my friends and mentors connect me with?

4. *Prioritize the people.* Look at the list of people you just made. You should have between 12 and 15 people on it. Ask yourself: How important is each of these people in helping me achieve my goal? Use Low, Moderate, or High to rank the people on your list and help you see who to start networking first with about your goal.

5. *Assess the quality of these relationships.* Start with relationships that you've decided are of High and Moderate importance. Remember to risk reaching out. There are three things you can do with your relationships: 1) *enrich* one that works well; 2) *repair* one that has gotten off track; 3) *start or rev up* one that is nonexistent or shaky.

Let's take a closer look at the three ways you can deal with your relationships:

Enrich a relationship. When you enrich a relationship, you deepen or reinforce it. When the relationship is already great, cultivate it further by showing appreciation and looking for new opportunities to help the other person. Recap what's gone well and appreciate that person's contribution. Acknowledge the level of trust. For example, you might say, "I know I can always count on you." Confirm that you're eager to help in any way you can.

Repair a relationship. Some relationships need fixing. Maybe you got off to a rocky start. Maybe the two of you had a misunderstanding. Maybe she stepped on your toes. Maybe you forgot to do what you promised. The relationship can get back on track if you acknowledge the situation, especially the part you played in the problem. Be prepared to appreciate the other person's qualities and skills and ask good questions to help you understand her point of view. Listen generously as you seek out positives and take ownership for repairing the relationship. You might say, "I know we've had some rocky times, but I'd like to turn over a new leaf and bring my best to working with you. I apologize for any part I had in creating the difficulties. I'd like to explore how we can start fresh and head off any misunderstandings in the future."

Start or rev up a relationship. Is there someone you'd like to enlist for your KeyNet, but have a minimal relationship with? Or maybe you and he have never even met? Maybe you need to get your boss's boss on board, but she works in Sydney, and you're based in Paris. Maybe the VP of Information Technology is new to the company—but crucial to your project. If that's the case, is there someone who can give you an introduction? Have you checked out the person's LinkedIn profile or company intranet profile to look for commonalities? Maybe you and she both went to the same university, or both have twins, or were both recently certified as coaches. It's up to you to risk reaching out. When you meet, ask good questions, listen for ways you can help, look for "the Give," and learn about the person's expertise, background, and talents. Listen to that person's challenges and find a resource, some information, or an introduction you can give to help with what he or she is up against.

Sometimes a relationship needs revving up. You may have lost touch with the person, and all it will take is having coffee together to renew the relationship. Maybe the relationship has plateaued: You've known each other—sort of —for years, but never have taken the next step. Schedule a meeting or arrange to sit with your contact at a professional association meeting or staff meeting. Once you're face-to-face, follow the suggestions for starting a relationship. The quality and usefulness of your relationships is up to you.

TIPS FOR CHOOSING YOUR KEYNET COLLABORATORS

Another way to think about who you'd like on your team for those big projects at work—or in life—is to think about the supporting roles people can play. You won't need someone in all of these roles, but enlisting people with at least some of these attributes will make your work a whole lot easier. Look for people with these kinds of talents and expertise:

- *The Brain:* Someone with hot-off-the-press information, best practices, know-how, experience, and enough knowledge about new technologies to see how they might help or hinder your project. Your subject-matter expert.

- *The Promoter:* Someone with market savvy who is in tune with the customer or end-user perspective.

- *The Creative:* Someone who knows about design, presentation, and color. This person can help you envision and build your brand, and maybe even create any online or print material you need to sell the idea.

- *The Global Citizen:* Someone who can cross cultures easily and understands the nuances of international communication.

- *The Influencer:* Someone who knows everybody; for example, a long-time employee. This person might accompany you to meet the board, or be part of the presentation team, if a "pitch" is required.

- *The Sponsor:* Someone who can authorize money and resources, marshal support, and pave the way.

- *The Wizard:* Someone who can make magic, is wildly creative, and who can come up with a stream of "out-of-the box" ideas. The innovator.

- *The Critic:* Someone who will "tell it like it is," ask the hard questions, give candid feedback, play devil's advocate, challenge your thinking.

- *The Cheerleader:* Someone whose energy is infectious, who's always upbeat, who will encourage you when you have a setback. Someone who can always find the pros when the cons build up.

- *The Guru:* Someone whose opinion you respect, who has a worldview and special wisdom that others respect.

- *The Sarge:* Someone who will hold you accountable, remind you of deadlines, set the pace, push you to excel.

- *The Wise Elder:* Someone who has experience working strategically and has pulled off many important projects. Invite this person to a private meeting to troubleshoot your plan.

- *The Novice:* Someone who is new to the organization or to this type of work, brings a fresh or young perspective, and will ask both naïve and cutting-edge questions.

- *The Heart:* Someone who is sensitive to the feelings and reactions of others, who knows how to appreciate and acknowledge others, and who is an excellent listener. Someone who strengthens the social cohesion of your KeyNet.

HOW THEY DID IT

Your roster will depend on what you want to accomplish. You won't need all of these types all of the time. Or you might decide you want two Cheerleaders, or three Sponsors. Deliberately seek out people unlike yourself—at different levels, in different functions, in different locations, in different organizations. Include people who do not have your biases, people you can learn from, and people who expand your capabilities. As you choose people, think roles, like Guru or Creative, or think Nets, so you don't miss anyone from your Four Nets that you want to include. The two examples below will give you ideas on how to put your KeyNet together.

Maria's KeyNet. Maria's goal was to start an affinity group for Hispanics. She set up a meeting with LaToya, the Chief Diversity Officer (a Sponsor, OrgNet), someone she'd already cultivated a relationship with. LaToya gave the go-ahead. Then, she invited several of her contacts to lunch in the private dining room. She asked her coworker Jose (an Influencer, WorkNet). She added Gabriela from another department (a Cheerleader, OrgNet), and Nancy, who worked for another company and was very involved with its Asian affinity group (a Wise Elder, ProNet), and new grad, new hire Camila (a Novice, OrgNet). At lunch, she introduced the idea and got their feedback. Based on their good ideas, she prepared a budget and timetable. LaToya approved them and shared another group's by-laws that made structuring the group easy. Maria brought the KeyNet back together to plan the first meeting and the publicity, and the affinity group was launched just four months later.

Looking back at the effort, Maria said, "It was so important to have Nancy's input. Her experience with a similar group was invaluable. And Camila gave us good advice about attracting the youngest employees and making sure they felt welcome."

- -

KeyNet members can play many roles to help your project succeed.

- -

Dan's KeyNet. As Dan, a director in charge of branch managers at a large bank, rose in seniority, he missed the direct contact he used to have with employees. Then, Molly, his favorite sister-in-law (a Brain, LifeNet), told him about her coaching certification program. Dan decided to investigate certification for himself. He remembered that two of his fellow members in the Chamber of Commerce were coaches. He interviewed Evan (a Guru, ProNet) and Harold (a Critic, ProNet) as well as his sister-in-law to decide which program to enroll in.

During the training program, he realized something: Coaching skills were exactly what he wanted his branch managers to use with the mortgage loan officers they supervised. He was convinced that creating a structure and a culture based on this very different kind of relationship would help his loan officers become even more successful.

Once he received his certification, Dan got busy on his plan to bring coaching to his bank. He located through his ProNet two coaches, Conrad and Jennifer, who worked at financial institutions similar to his and interviewed them. Then he put together his KeyNet to help him lay the groundwork for getting buy-in from his branch managers. His KeyNet included Martin (a Wise Elder, OrgNet), Anna (an Influencer, OrgNet), and Conner (a Sarge, OrgNet). He strategized with these people about how to present the idea to Yvonne, his boss (a Sponsor, OrgNet). His KeyNet suggested he set up a conference call with Conrad and Jennifer, so they could tell Yvonne how coaching was working at their companies. He also invited Yvonne to a professional meeting for coaches, so she could learn more about how coaching works in other organizations. Just 11 months after he became a certified coach, Dan launched the bank's pilot program.

Looking back at the contributions of his KeyNet members, Dan said, "We had four meetings. After each one, I felt energized and clear about what I had to do. Martin was such a good sounding board, and Conner was always urging me on. I couldn't have done it without my KeyNet."

■ ■ ■

The Four Nets is a concept that promotes diversity and balance in your networks. Now that you can see where your contacts come from, you're ready to learn specific skills for developing those relationships you have with people from all of your Nets.

4

·····················

Develop Trusting
Relationships

Strategic Connections: Reach Out in the Community
At a large bank, executives from a three-state region got together. They weren't satisfied with the results from their relationship managers. Those people had been told, "Reach out to entrepreneurs." But the RMs were struggling to sign up small businesses as clients. One executive said, "I've seen how they approach potential customers. They say, 'Hi, I'm Bob. Here's my card, in case you need any banking services.'" Another chimed in, "They join organizations, but don't know how to get visible and position the bank and our services in such a way that we get the business." A third agreed, "They don't know what to do and say to make sure that contacts become clients."

AS THESE BANK managers found out, networking isn't just appearing; it's interacting to build trusting relationships. This chapter focuses on Competency 4, establishing trust in relationships. Without trust, relationships cannot develop. As you teach people about yourself and learn about others, you move through six Stages of Trust. Understanding these Stages will help you decide on behaviors that are professional—not too pushy and not too passive. You'll be able to determine what Stage of Trust you've reached with the contacts you have in your Four Nets, and you'll know what to do and say at each Stage of the trust-building process to intensify those relationships.

Relationships are the foundation of success, whether in the organization or as you build your career. As relationships multiply and strengthen throughout the organization and outside, their power becomes evident in new ideas and ways of doing things, in new or expanded work from clients, and in new leads or opportunities.

Teach People to Trust You

Everybody agrees with the statement, "People want to do business with people they trust." Yet we've all had an experience like this: You're at a networking event and someone comes up to you and says, "Hi, I'm Eric. I sell three-year global mobile plans. Do you want one?" It's this kind of "going for the jugular" that gives networking a bad name. You don't know or trust Eric enough to do business with him.

Remember the old saying: "It's not *what* you know, it's *who* you know"? That's only partly true. Sure, what you know is important. It's your expertise, your knowledge, what you get paid for, the value you bring to the table. Who you know is important, too. Those are the people you call when you are looking for an idea, a resource, a referral, or a little support.

But just as in important as *what* you know and *who* you know is *who knows you*. Does Stacey know you so well that, when something comes into her life, you pop into her head, and she says to herself, "Oh, I've got to send this to Sean." How many people know you that well?

Trust happens as you teach others about your Character and Competence and learn about theirs. We give specific meanings to the words "Character" and "Competence." Character refers to the constellation of positive personal qualities, revealed in all you do and say, that assures people you are trustworthy; Competence refers to the breadth and depth of your expertise, revealed in all you do and say, that assures people you are trustworthy.

So how long does it take to develop trust? Our Contacts Count research shows that it takes six to eight conversations in which you prove you can be trusted and take note of what contacts do and say to decide if *they* can be trusted. So see if you can create six encounters:

- Six times when you come into contact—ideally face to face, but perhaps by phone, or via the Internet.

- Six times when they get to see your Character and Competence, and you see theirs.

- Six times when you teach them what to come to you for, what you're looking for, what you're good at, what they can count on you for—and you learn the same about them.

- Six times when they learn enough about you that they can introduce you and talk about your talents and achievements.

- Six times when you have a chance to become comfortable with each other.

. . . .

Show and tell to teach others about your character.

. . . .

TEACH CHARACTER

To teach your contacts about your Character, find ways to show that you:

- Do what you say you will do.

- Meet deadlines.

- Go for the win-win solution.

- Treat everyone you meet fairly.

- Be unfailingly reliable.

- Speak well of people even when they are not present.

- Come from a position of abundance, not scarcity.

- Move from competition to collaboration.

- When something goes wrong, make it right and compensate generously for your mistake.

- Go the extra mile.

- Respect other people's time and possessions.

- Say, "Thank you!"

To believe in your Character, your contacts must see you in action and hear you tell stories about how you've handled various situations.

If you tell Jane you'll call her on Tuesday at 2 P.M., pick up the phone at 1:59. That's how you teach her that you'll do what you say you'll do.

If you promise Beth you'll come up with 10 items for the public television fund-raising auction by December 5, provide a dozen by December 1. That's how you'll teach her that you meet deadlines, are reliable, and always go the extra mile.

If you want Joseph to know you're a stickler for details, tell about the corporate magazine you edit and the multiple processes you have to check that every name is spelled correctly and all details in the articles are accurate before it goes to press.

If you want Freda, your boss, to notice that you're an innovative thinker, show her how your work as chair of the program committee doubled attendance at your Employee Resource Group.

If you want to teach Joe that you're a good organizer, tell about compiling information from 12 board members and their committees to help your professional association chapter win the Chapter of the Year contest.

TEACH COMPETENCE

To teach your contacts about your Competence, find ways to show that you:

- Have earned the proper credentials.

- Stay at the leading edge of your profession.

- Win praise and awards from your peers.

- Take lifelong learning seriously.

- Are cited as an expert in the trade press or in the mass media.

- Teach or mentor others.

- Consult with others to share your expertise.

- Write for publications or speak in public.

- Do the job right—the first time.

- Are happy to discuss your procedures and processes with clients and customers.

- Handle "the little stuff" with care.

- Follow through to be sure that your work meets—or exceeds—expectations.

To believe in your Competence, your contacts must see you in action and hear you tell stories about how you've handled various situations.

If you want Donna to know you keep up with the latest changes in your field, tell her about the amazing course on creating website surveys you just took.

If you want to teach Jeffrey that you're a mentor, tell him about the innovative way the mentoring program at your organization is structured and how much you're getting out of your work with younger staffers.

> *Your actions and anecdotes provide evidence of your Competence.*

If you want Georgia to know you're an expert in your field, send her a copy of the article you wrote for an industry publication.

To build trust, make sure people know your capabilities and are confident in your ability to perform. It's unreasonable to expect that people who don't know you will be comfortable giving you referrals or suggesting you for special assignments. They have no idea what your special areas of expertise are and have not known you long enough to be sure you will come through. Learn about your contacts' Character and Competence the same way. Pay attention to what they say and do.

Move Through the Six Stages of Trust

There's a misconception about networking these days. Because of the binary nature of social media tools—you're "friended" or "linked" or not—it's easy to assume that you either have—or do not have—a relationship.

The reality is more complex than that. Look at Figure 4–1, The Six Stages of Trust.

Make a list of 10 people you know. Include a variety of people from all of your Nets: people you know well and people you have just met; people you used to know, but have lost touch with; coworkers, clients, customers, or vendors; people from a professional association or community organization; people from your life outside of work. Keep these people in mind as you learn about the Stages in the paragraphs that follow. See if you can figure out where you are with each of them.

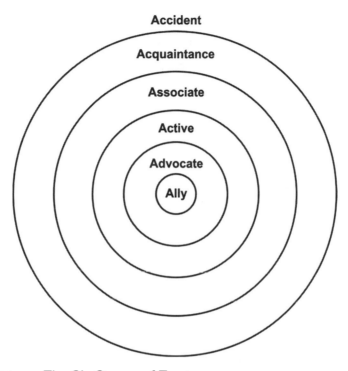

FIGURE 4–1. *The Six Stages of Trust*

Accidents. In your lifetime, you will bump into thousands of people. They are Accidents. Given the reality of casual, unplanned, random encounters, you'll probably never run into them again. Circumstances have brought you together for some period of time. So you talk to each other—as you stand in line for tickets to the hit play, in the doctor's office waiting room, when you are in seat 14A and she is in 14B on the airplane. You can create relationships with these people—if you decide to reach out and stay in touch. Often though, after a pleasant conversation, nothing happens.

Acquaintances. People you don't see regularly, but could find again are Acquaintances. You meet Acquaintances through the people you know. For example, you're at a meeting in a client's office, and the client introduces you to his colleague who works in another department. Or you go to a barbecue at your cousin's house, and you meet your cousin's neighbor. You could find the client's colleague again, and you could find your cousin's neighbor again if you wanted to. Because Acquaintances are people you don't see regularly, building a relationship depends on your desire to do so and your ability to reach out with intention. You may be granted some trust because of your relationship with the person who brought you together, but you'll still have to prove your trustworthiness for the relationship to grow.

Acquaintances are valuable because they can connect you with new circles. They're especially useful when, for example, you are job hunting. You can think of them as "untapped assets."

• •

Acquaintances are bridges to new circles.

• •

Associates. People who have joined the groups you've joined are Associates. Because you belong to the same group you see each other regularly. That happens when you both:

- Work for the same organization.

- Belong to the same professional association.

- Join the same networking organization at work or outside of work.

- Attend the same church or synagogue or mosque.

- Go to the same fitness center.

- Take part in alumni activities at the school you attended.

- Enjoy a leisure-time activity together.

Because you and your Associates belong to the same group, you have an implied permission to seek each other out. And there may be a presumption that because you both are Tech alums, you are both *probably* persons of good character and ability. However, you'll still have to check each other out.

Actives. People with whom you exchange valuable information, resources, or introductions are Actives. Relationships that start out at the Accident, Acquaintance, or Associate Stage all can evolve to the Active Stage. You and your contact become Actives when you get into activity, swapping ideas, providing something of interest. So pour your energy into having a rich conversation—one that uncovers a commonality or a need. You might tell an Active about a favorite restaurant, a website, or an article. She might invite you to an event. You're giving to each other in a variety of ways. You're gathering information about each other and have each other's phone numbers and email addresses. You're beginning to know enough about her, and she about you, to be useful to each other.

Whether you realize it consciously or not, at this Stage of the relationship-building process, you're looking for two things in the person you've become Active with. If you see these two things, exhibited in everything the person says and does, then you'll want more activity with her; if you don't see these two things, you'll walk the other direction the next time you see her. You won't pursue the relationship. What are these two things you're looking for? Character and Competence!

Advocates. People who have come to believe in each other's Character and Competence are Advocates. You know that your Advocates will speak well of you, and they know that you will help them. You have developed a high degree of trust with each other. Your antenna is up for information and resources for your Advocates. And they, likewise, feed you opportunities. You enjoy promoting them to others. Advocates seek each other out and say things like:

"Hey, I've got an idea for you."

"I ran across something I want to send to you. I'll email it to you."

"I met someone who's very interested in your service. How about if the three of us meet for lunch on Friday?"

Being an Advocate is a risky business. Notice the phrases people use. An Advocate must overcome his natural caution in order to "go out on a limb" for you, "stick his neck out" for you, and "put his good name on the line" for you. What scary metaphors! So take seriously the gigantic leap of trust that someone has made when he becomes your Advocate. Consciously show your Character and Competence—and look for telling behaviors in others, so you don't tarnish your credibility by advocating for someone you don't know well enough to endorse.

Trust is of special interest to Alex Pentland, Director of Massachusetts Institute of Technology's Human Dynamics Lab. He studies what conditions and behaviors create a flow of ideas. In his book *Social Physics: How Good Ideas Spread*, he defines trust like this: "Trust is the expectation of continued, stable exchange value" in a relationship. It's a measure of the risk you will take when you interact with someone. In fact, Pentland goes on to describe a study in which he was able to actually predict who would do things like loan someone $100 or loan someone their car—so-called "risky" behaviors—by counting the number of successful exchanges the two had had in the past. This is why moving from Active to Advocate is best accomplished by spending more time with someone. Assuming you do and say things that show your Character and Competence, trust will grow the more you "hang out" together.

As trust develops, risk recedes.

Allies. Think of Allies as the people who are on the board of directors of your life. Did you know you have a board of directors of your life? You may not have officially appointed them, but these are the people you turn to:

- When you need advice or support.

- When you want to commiserate, or celebrate.

- When you have an important decision to make.

- When you need to talk with a trusted friend in confidence.

Allies care about your success and happiness as a human being. They are involved in all aspects of your life, both personal and professional. They will go to extraordinary lengths to help you succeed. You're going through life together. It's not necessary or practical to have lots and lots of Allies. You'll cultivate this Stage of Trust with just a few special people you know you can count on. The relationship hinges on the trust and respect you have for each other, not the amount of time you spend together. But you certainly do make time for each other.

Allies are experts on you, your business, your career, your needs, your aspirations, and your vision. They know where you've been and where you're headed—and they want to help you get there! They are your senior advisors, and you are theirs. Because you talk about core life and business issues, confidentiality is a ground rule of your relationship. These are the people you turn to for sage advice—on how to climb the corporate ladder, on whether it's time to open a branch office in Denver, on how to deal with a difficult client, even on whether or not to adopt a child. Allies commiserate with you when the going gets rough and celebrate with you when success is sweet.

Renew Dormant Ties

In their Spring 2011 *MIT Sloan Management Review* article, "The Power of Reconnection: How Dormant Ties Can Surprise You," Professors Daniel Levin, Jorge Walter, and Keith Murnighan explain what happens when you go back to contacts you've lost touch with. They asked 200 executives to contact dormant ties (people they hadn't talked with in three years or more) to get advice on a work project.

The executives were skeptical. They also were told to ask current contacts the same questions. The results were startling:

1. Long-lost contacts gave more new information than current ones, who were likely to have access to the same information, hold many of the same viewpoints, and know the same people as the executives.

2. When reconnecting with long-lost contacts, it wasn't like starting over. The trust that was built years ago remained.

Think about your dormant relationships—people you used to know, used to work with, used to socialize with. Make a list; choose the five you remember most clearly or most fondly. Contact them. They can be much more important than you might have thought.

> *Inactive relationships are surprisingly valuable.*

Don't be reluctant to reengage with these people. The relationships can often be reactivated. Make a phone call and say, "Isn't it time for our annual—or once-every-three-years—lunch?" You'll both benefit from reconnecting.

Analyze Your Contacts

Go back to that list of 10 people you made at the beginning of our discussion of the six Stages of Trust. Decide what Stage of Trust you've reached with each person on your list. Assuming that your list of 10 is representative of all the people you know, what does it tell you about how you need to expand and develop your networks? Are you in the right groups to meet the type of Associates who can someday become Actives and Advocates? Do you have enough Advocates? What ideas do you have about next steps you might take if you want more of a relationship with some of the 10 on your list? If you were to make an even broader list of the people you know, would there be a good mix of people from different parts of your life? Think about where these 10 people fit in your Four Nets. Do you have Actives and Advocates in all your Nets? Sometimes people notice that they have only Associate Stage relationships with the people in their ProNet, for example.

RATE YOUR RELATIONSHIPS

Choose someone on your list of 10 and use this quiz to figure out where you are with that person. If you don't know the answer to a question, then the answer is "No."

Does my contact:

1. Demonstrate knowing my face and my name by coming up to me, saying hello, and introducing me accurately to others?

2. Know me well enough to recognize me "out of context" in a new setting?

3. Know several ways to contact me?

4. Recognize my name instantly when I call?

5. In conversation, explore commonalities and needs?

6. Accurately describe what I do?

7. Give vivid examples of what I do?

8. Know that I am good at what I do and cite reasons why my work is superior?

9. Know of some independent verification of my expertise—an award, certification, third-party endorsement?

10. Respond quickly to requests from me?

11. Regularly send me valuable information and resources?

12. Know what kinds of people can use my expertise and is on the lookout for them?

13. Always speak well of me to others and pass my name along?

14. Tell me the truth, keep confidences, and have my best interests at heart?

15. Bring me into all areas of his/her life over a long period of time?

When did you begin to answer "no"? Noticing that will help you pinpoint what you want to be sure to tell—or ask—the next time you see this person. As an intentional networker, you'll be aware of what kinds of things you'd like to teach your contacts in each encounter. This quiz highlights our finding that it often takes six or eight contacts with someone before she knows who you are, has learned what you do, and has the evidence she needs to begin to trust you. Once that trust is established, you might be in touch once a week or once a year, depending on the relationship.

As you took the quiz did you notice that the questions reflect the Stages of Trust? For instance, questions 5–7 are what Actives focus on; 8–13 are what Advocates do for each other; and 14 and 15 are what make Ally relationships so special.

This quiz not only helps you figure out where you are with someone, it also helps you figure out what you need to teach as you take the next step.

USE TIME TO GAUGE TRUST

Another way to determine the Stage you've reached with someone is the amount of time it takes for that person to respond to your request. If you are an Associate (you belong to the same group), you can look for a response within the week. If you are an Active (you've begun to exchange valuable information), you can look for a response within three or four days. If you are an Advocate (you've convinced your contact of your Character and Competence), you can expect a response within 48 hours. If you are an Ally, you'll hear back in hours.

Notice that your response time to contacts in the various Stages will be about the same. Trust speeds responsiveness. That's a particularly valuable result for building strong networking relationships.

> ### Staying in Touch
>
> "When I met with my coworker Tom, he complained that for months he'd been trying to get some information from the IT department—with no results. 'I don't even know who to talk to over there,' he said.
>
> "I said, 'I'll be right back' and excused myself from the meeting. Finding Charlie in IT, I asked, 'Can you send the survey data to Tom?' Charlie said, 'Sure!' and sent the information on the spot.
>
> "I went back to the meeting and said with a smile, 'You'll find it in your email when you get back to your office.'
>
> "Tom looked incredulous. 'How did you *do* that??? And in five minutes! I've been trying to get that out of them for months.'
>
> "I said, 'It didn't take five minutes. It took five years. That's how long I've known Charlie. I worked with him on a project and made sure to keep in touch.'"

Next Steps: Consider the Risk and Value

Before you decide on a good next step with someone, consider the risk involved—to you and to the other person. Take a moment to gauge the potential value involved—to you and to the other person. Risk is what one stands to lose; value is what one stands to gain. There are low-risk and high-risk next steps, and there are low-value and high-value next steps; every next step is some combination of low/high risk and low/high value.

Jessie's leadership development program had won awards. She'd been asked to write an article about the challenges organizations face when they design and launch programs like hers. She asked Bob, an

Active, who was just starting a similar program, to tell her about his experience. She offered to share her expertise in return for the interview and the chance to quote him. That's a high-value/low-risk next step—a win-win for both Jessie and Bob.

* * *

Before taking the next step, consider the risk and value.

* * *

Here are some things to keep in mind as you think through your next step. There's not much to recommend a low-value next step. You might rethink whatever you had in mind. And don't automatically reject a high-risk next step just because it's risky.

A *low-risk* next step:

- Asks for something your contact is probably ready, willing and able to give.

- Is not time sensitive. You don't need it yesterday.

- Is easy for your contact to do.

A *high-risk* next step:

- Asks for something that will be difficult for your contact to give.

- Requires the expenditure of significant time, money, and/or effort.

- Could put your contact in an awkward situation.

A *low-value* next step:

- Doesn't significantly move the relationship toward the next Stage.

- Doesn't provide a tangible result or outcome.

- Might waste your contact's time.

A *high-value* next step:

- Teaches about your Character and Competence.

- Impacts favorably on your contact's life, well-being, or work.

- Positions your contact favorably among his or her colleagues.

PLAN THE NEXT STEP

Keeping in mind risk and value, you're ready to decide what to do if you'd like to have more of a relationship with someone. Here are some options.

For Accidents and Acquaintances, ask yourself, "What might this person bring to my network? Would he give me access to new circles? Would she introduce me to new ideas, or diverse groups of people? What might we have in common? Could I gain new perspectives by knowing this person? Would I enjoy knowing this person?" And of course, ask yourself, "Would knowing this person in some way bring me closer to accomplishing my job-specific goals and contribute more to my organization's success?"

Here are some examples:

- Find a reason to introduce yourself. Say, "I notice you're reading one of my favorite books. How do you like it?"

- Propose another meeting. Say, "I'd like to hear more about your project. Got time for coffee on Friday?"

- Exchange contact information. Say, "Your project sounds very interesting. Here's my card. I'd like to have yours, too. Let's stay in touch."

- Invite him to join a group you belong to. "I get a lot out of the monthly meetings of the users group. Would you like to come to the next one?"

- And, of course, be ready to teach your name and be ready to answer the "What do you do?" question. (See Chapters 5 and Chapter 7 for more information on mastering these skills.)

For Associates, ask yourself, "What do we have in common? How are we different? What's her role in the organization we both are members of? How can I become known to her? Are there ways I can show her my Character and Competence? How can I help her? What is she hoping to get out of belonging to this group or working here?"

Here are some examples:

- Ask a colleague to introduce you with a few words about what you do or what she thinks you two might have in common.

- Respond to a comment your Associate made in a speech, in the newsletter, or online.

- Join your Associate in some activity or committee, so you have multiple opportunities to get to know each other.

- Send a note of congratulations when you notice that he's done something that is especially innovative or remarkable. Say, "Congrats on landing that new client!"

- Appreciate something about your Associate. Say, "I learned so much from you about trends in our industry when I heard you speak at the conference."

- Show support for her initiatives by attending an event your Associate is in charge of.

- Find a commonality. "I heard you lived in London. I did too." Or, "Tom told me you're interested in helping our engineers improve their business development skills. I am too."

For Actives, ask yourself, "What is she interested in? Would she like me to introduce her to someone? Does she know someone I might like to know? What do we have in common? What circles is she involved in that I'm not? What interests do we share? What stories can I tell to teach her about my expertise? What activities can I suggest, so we can continue to get to know each other? What are several things I know about her that will help me introduce her enthusiastically and accurately to others? What's coming up in her life that I might be able to help her with?"

Here are some examples:

- Teach him what to come to you for by telling casual, conversational, and brief stories or examples of the kinds of things you're working on or interested in.

- Ask good questions, such as, "What are you excited about?" or "What trends do you see?" Then listen generously to see what resources or information you might offer.

- Propose a meeting. Say, "Want me to come by and pick you up for the event? Parking is so hard downtown and riding together will give us a chance to talk."

- If you make a mistake (call her by the wrong name or forget to do something you said you'd do), apologize. Be sure to seek out *more* interaction, so the mistake fades into the background and what stands out are your Character and Competence.

- Look for news online or in print that she might like to know about and send it to her.

- Appreciate things he does. "Thanks for chairing that committee." Or, "So glad you're going to be on the panel." Or, "I appreciated your encouragement last week."

- Introduce her with enthusiasm in a sentence or two that makes it clear what she and the other person might have in common. Say, "Don, I especially want you to meet Chihiro, because I remember you said you're working on the new product launch. Chihiro has lots of experience with that sort of thing." Or, "Eric, I want you to meet Bill. Bill's also the father of twins—and just started a public relations consulting firm."

- Show that you remember what she tells you about projects, interests, and challenges by sending useful information and resources.

- Ask your contact to join you in an activity you think he will enjoy or profit from.

- Teach him what you're looking for. Say, "I'm looking for advice about working abroad." Or, "Keep me in mind if you hear about any workshops on negotiating."

For Advocates, ask yourself, "How can I keep current about his skills and talents, so I can send him the right opportunities? Am I keeping him up to date about what I'm doing, and asking him to update me? Am I on the lookout for ways to send her clients, opportunities, and valuable information? Do I know someone that my Advocate would benefit from meeting? How can I help him succeed?"

Here are some examples:

- Ask questions to update the information and examples you have to pass along to others. Say, "What are two or three things you've worked on recently that I can tell others when I'm talking about you?"

- Refer him to others. Say, "Hugh, I'd like to give your name to my boss. He's looking for an executive coach—just the kind of person your firm supplies."

- Introduce her to others. Say, "Alice, can you come to lunch on Wednesday? I've invited a couple of others I think you'd like to meet because of your new venture."

- Make yourself useful. Ask, "What kinds of challenges do you foresee in the next six months? Maybe I know people who can help."

For Allies, ask yourself, "How can I confirm and enrich our relationship? Am I keeping confidences? Do I help her celebrate? Am I there when he needs a shoulder to lean on? Do I sing her praises far and wide? Do I respond to calls and requests immediately? Do I find ways to remind him of his best values, traits, and gifts? Do I tell her how much I appreciate our friendship and all the ways she supports me?"

Here are some examples:

- Every once in a while, in conversation, recap your relationship. Appreciate the ways you've helped each other and recount the good times and bad times you've been through. Say, "I was so nervous about taking that new job. Your support and advice really got me through some rough times in the first few weeks."

- Appreciate his skills and talents. Say, "I admire how you pull together mountains of data and present it in a way that helps people make sense of it all." Or, "You have such a talent for helping people resolve their conflicts. Have you ever thought about that as a career path?"

- Express the trust you feel in the relationship. Say, "I know I can always count on you to be straight with me and tell me the truth even when I might not want to hear it."

- Look to the future. Say, "Let's be sure to support each other as our parents begin to age and need more help. I can already see that's going to be difficult."

- Confirm your willingness to help. Say, "You know you can count on me to do everything I can do to make the transition you're coping with easier for you."

- Challenge him to take risks, have courage, grow, and change. Say, "I can imagine moving overseas for a year can be a bit daunting. But I'm confident you can make the most of the experience."

- Ask questions that go deeper. Say, "What is the best thing in your life right now? What's missing? What's next for you?"

- Talk about your relationship as something that you're creating together. Say, "I appreciate the way you really listen to me. Suddenly whatever's bothering me begins to looks a lot better."

THREE THINGS TO REMEMBER

As you think about the Stages of Trust and how you'd like to develop your relationships, here are some important ideas to keep in mind:

1. *You can't **make** a contact move to the next Stage.* There's a thin line between being manipulative and intentional. If you try to get someone to advocate for you before he or she is assured of your Character and Competence, you emit a kind of predatory energy. People don't like that. You can't "turn Jim into an Advocate," but you can say and do things that will make it more likely that the relationship will grow. When you give something to Jim, you become an Active. When he reciprocates, he joins you in that Stage. When you recommend Jim for a special assignment, you've become his Advocate. When he nominates you for an award he becomes your Advocate.

2. *Your goal is not to become Allies with everyone you meet.* Being and remaining at the Active or Advocate Stage with someone can be very beneficial on its own. Be intentional about which relationships you choose to develop.

3. *Acquaintances can be more valuable than you might think.* They provide bridges to diverse contacts and circles you otherwise might not be able to access.

Tuning in to the Stage of Trust you enjoy with someone helps you avoid asking for too much too soon . . . or too little too late. It would probably be inappropriate if you asked someone you just met to sponsor your new initiative. On the other hand, if you never reach out to people to let them know what you're looking for or how they can help, then you're underusing your network.

You'll have fleeting contact with thousands of Accidents, Acquaintances, and Associates in your lifetime. You'll have an Active relationship with many people. Hopefully quite a few will become Advocates. A special few will become Allies.

Relationships don't happen at the click of a mouse. They happen when you invest the time to teach people to trust you. As you use your trust-building/relationship-developing skills, you power up the Network-Oriented Workplace.

Frequently Asked Questions

Q: *I've made some incredible contacts with Accidents. I got a $50,000 training contract because I said hello to a fellow passenger in the van from the airport to the hotel. Why do you say it takes six to eight contacts?*

A: Making a magical connection with someone you meet on the fly (pun intended) is great. And it's true that sometimes trust seems instantaneous. But as a rule, it takes longer to teach and learn about each other's Character and Competence.

Q: *Can customers and clients become Advocates and Allies? I guess we became Actives when I worked for them but that was four years ago. I haven't been in touch recently.*

A: Sure they can. Reconnect with your former clients, using the process outlined in this chapter to develop the relationships.

Q: *When I looked at my 10 people and tried to place them in the Stages of Trust model, all were Associates. What am I doing wrong?*

A: This situation is typical for younger networkers who haven't had the time—or perhaps the need—to build networks. First, you may simply have been thinking of groups you belong to as you made your list of 10. That would have led you to write down mostly Associates. Second, you may need to do more than join organizations. You may need to work at your networking to deepen those relationships.

Q: *I thought of 10 people, but my best contacts are my friends. Do my friends fit on that model? Or are they outside?*

A: Again, this situation is typical of networkers early in their careers. They're still hanging around with college buddies or people they grew up with. It's great to think of friends as networking contacts. Have conversations with them about keeping your antennas up for each other, so that you can provide opportunities for each other. And certainly, when you become Allies with someone, they become friends because you have shared your personal and career goals. It's wise, however, to cultivate contacts strategically—to specialize a bit—so that you meet people in your career field or profession.

Q: *I have people that I think of as Actives because I've done something for them, but they never do anything for me. How can I not only move to the next Stage with them, but also be sure that the relationship is mutually beneficial?*

A: Think about these people as you answer the questions on the Rate Your Relationships quiz. Perhaps you haven't taught them what you're looking for and how they might be helpful. Next time you meet have a couple of stories to tell them, so that they can better appreciate your Character and Competence. If you continue to feel that they aren't reciprocating, have a conversation in which you recount some of the things you done for them and say, "Here's how you could help me." If that doesn't work, you may decide to shrug and say to yourself, "I'm going to keep giving because I believe in it." Or you may decide to spend your time relating to people who do give back.

Q: *There's an Associate of mine that I don't want to have a relationship with at all. He's not a person whose ethics I admire. But he keeps calling and wanting to get together. What should I do?*

A: Be busy when he calls, very busy.

Q: *I think I have all Advocates and Allies in my network.*

A: People typically overestimate the amount of information their contacts have about them. And people usually haven't focused on teaching people to trust them. Check out what your contacts know by having conversations and asking them, for example, to give a vivid example of what you do. If they can't or you don't like what they say, tell them stories. They'll be likely to remember those examples. Ask yourself if you are suffering from Tired Network Syndrome. You may have been at it so long, that you do have a cadre of well-established relationships. On the other hand, do you have networking needs that they are unable to fulfill—new passions in your life that your current contacts are not connecting with? If so, deliberately set out to join some new groups and meet some people who share your new interests.

> *People overestimate what their contacts know about them.*

Q: *How much time does it take to develop and nurture a relationship with an Ally?*

A: Lots. Because you are so in tune, you may be tempted to cut back on the time you spend with these valuable contacts. Be sure that you do set aside a regular time to get together, perhaps dinner once a month. Challenge yourself to find some way that you can contribute to their success every time you meet. Listen generously, be seriously curious, and swap stories. Then you'll be able to profit from—and continue to enjoy—those relationships for years to come.

5

....

Increase Your
Social Acumen

SUJATA UNDERSTANDS that her sales team's success depends on what happens face to face. Remember the line that movie director Woody Allen made famous? His maxim was, "80 percent of success is showing up." Sujata doesn't buy into the idea that if her people just go to the event, the other 20 percent will take care of itself. In fact, she said she'd flip the numbers: 20 percent of success is showing up, and 80 percent is knowing what to do and say once you get there.

What Is Social Acumen?

Competency 5, increasing social acumen, shows you how to make the most of every moment you have with people. As you increase your social acumen, you'll understand how to make the most of the rituals we go through as we connect with each other. You'll have the impetus to connect with more people throughout your organization and beyond. The skills you'll learn here will assure that you make a positive first impression and get new relationships off to a good start. Will you manage the meet-and-greet rituals with comfort and confidence, or ignore the "netiquette" and just muddle through?

> *Manage meet-and-greet rituals with comfort and confidence.*

This chapter takes you from "hello" to "goodbye." You'll get tips on how to remember names, teach your name, join groups of people who are already talking, and end conversations with the future in mind. And you'll learn more about likeability—what it is, why it's important in the business world, and how to increase yours.

The Name Exchange

In our workshops, people are amazed when they realize how many seconds they usually spend on introductions. Count the seconds the next time you exchange names with someone. Most people spend only four or five seconds! No wonder our Contacts Count surveys show that 97 percent of the respondents say, "I'm no good at remembering names." You're asking the impossible of yourself to think that you can learn someone's name—and teach that person your name—in only a few seconds. To recognize the true importance of the Name Exchange, reframe it as teaching and learning, not just saying and hearing. In networking, learning someone's name is the first step in the trust-building process. Slow down. Linger longer over names.

• •

The average name exchange takes four or five seconds.

• •

LEARN SOMEONE'S NAME

When someone says her name, don't immediately reply with your own. Instead, focus first on learning hers. Here are three ways to do that. These ideas are so simple you may be tempted to dismiss them. Don't do that! Train yourself to use these steps every time you meet someone. They work.

Step #1. Repeat the first name. Say, "It's nice to meet you, Jennifer." You may think that you already do that, but our research indicates that repeating the name happens only about 25 percent of the time. Train yourself to do it *every* time. Then, hang on to Jennifer's name long enough to introduce her to at least one other person. Whether you make that introduction 30 minutes later or three hours later, Jennifer will appreciate that you bothered to remember her name. It's a sign of respect to learn someone's name. Notice that so far you've only focused on her first name. That's fine. It's the tried-and-true principle of "divide and conquer." Learn the person's first name first.

Step #2. Ask for the last name again or confirm it. Say, "And your last name was . . .?" Or, "Tell me your last name again." Or, "Did you say your last name is O'Grady?" The person will repeat her last name. She'll say, very clearly, "It's O'Grady." One problem with the old Name Exchange ritual is that people are so used to saying their names that they run through them too quickly, mashing their first and last names together. When you ask for the last name by itself, your contact will say it more distinctly.

Step #3. Ask a question or make a comment about the person's name. Comment either on the first name or the last name. It's a chance for you to say the name again. Here are some suggestions:

"Do you like to be called Jenny or Jennifer?"

"O'Grady sounds like it might be Irish. Is that right?"

TEACH YOUR NAME

Even if you think your name is easy to remember, teaching it is an essential social acumen skill. Be ready to use these three techniques to help people learn your name.

Step #1. Give 'em a double dip. Say your first name twice. "I'm Bob, Bob . . . Schmidt." Remember Tom Hanks as Forrest Gump in the movie by the same name? He always said his first name twice: "I'm Forrest, Forrest Gump."

Step #2. Separate and articulate. Say your first name, then pause, then *pronounce* your last name crisply and distinctly. "I'm Bob, Bob (pause) Schmidt." You're used to saying your name, but others aren't used to hearing it, so make sure you don't run it all together. Especially if you think your name may be unfamiliar to the other person, slow down. Remember, when you're introducing yourself, you're not just saying your name; you're *teaching* your name.

Step #3. Make your name memorable. Say something about your name to help the person you're talking with remember it. Spelling your name is one way to do that. People will visualize the letters in their mind. Nancy Mann says, "It's Mann with two 'Ns.' I'm the only the only woman who's a Mann who's in real estate in Kansas City."

Here are a few more good examples that help people "see" the spelling:

"Hi, I'm Kevin, Kevin Janes. Like Jones, but with an 'A.'"

"Hi, I'm Liam, Liam Lawrence. Liam is 'mail' spelled backwards."

"Hi, I'm Collin, Collin Morrissey: with two 'Ls,' two 'Rs,' and two 'Ss.'"

Another way to teach your name is to give a tip to help others remember it. Do any of these examples give you an idea about how teach your name?

"Hi, I'm Kabwayi Kabongo. Think of 'cowboy' and 'bongos.'"

"Hi, I'm Wade, Wade Johnson. Wade, like wade in the water."

"Hi, I'm Lawrence, Lawrence Brown. I'm named Lawrence after my grandfather—he still leads our engineering firm."

"Hi, I'm Louise, Louise Poppei. Even though the spelling might not look like it, you say my last name like the flower—poppy."

"Hi, I'm Linda, Linda Watson. I'm way down at the end of the alphabet—Watson."

If you meet someone who says, "Oh, I never can remember names," that's your cue to say, "You can remember mine. Here's how: It's Rayna, Rayna Jaynes. Rayna because I'm named after my dad, Ray. And both my names have a 'Y' in the middle."

Since the whole idea is to slow down and interrupt that Ping-Pong game we play as we exchange names—you give your name and I give mine right back—anything you can do to spend time on teaching and learning names will pay off in the long run. People often ask Georgia, "Were you named for the state?" Although she's explained many times that, yes, she was born there, she doesn't mind because she knows that many interesting conversations and connections have come out of sharing that bit of information. If you just say, "Hi, I'm Linda." And she just says, "Hi, I'm Georgia," there's nothing to build the conversation around.

Include as part of your growing networker identity the idea that you're good with names. Since only three in a hundred people say they are, you'll stand out as someone who's serious about connecting.

DEAL SKILLFULLY WITH FORGOTTEN NAMES

Has this ever happened to you? You see someone across the room and think to yourself, "I *know* that person. What is her name?" This is not an age-related problem; it's a brain-overload problem. Let's face it, you know hundreds of people—coworkers, clients, colleagues, cousins—so the expectation that you'll never forget a name is unrealistic.

Here are four things to do if you experience that awkward moment:

1. Walk confidently up to the person, shake hands, and say, "I remember you. Good to see you again. I'm Craig, Craig Weinstock." You're banking on the ritual: When you give your name, the other person will most likely say his name. You've shown that you remember him and acknowledged that you've met before.

2. If you recall the situation in which you met or a topic you discussed, say, "Hi! We met at the conference, and I remember you told me about your new job." Maybe his name will come to you as the conversation gets going. Or maybe someone else will come up and call him by name. Or if you and he decide to exchange business cards, you'll have his name forever.

3. Ask her name with lots of energy and enthusiasm. Say, "Tell me your name again. I remember you!" That's what people want to know—that you remember them. They will forgive that you've momentarily forgotten the name. And then be sure to give your name in case it's a two-way memory lapse!

4. Before you approach, ask a colleague to remind you of the forgotten name. Say, "Jerry, I know I've met that guy over there with the red tie. Remind me of his name."

Above all, if you've forgotten someone's name, do avoid this scenario. You see her across the room. You make eye contact, then hang your head, slowly shuffle over with a discouraged look on your face, limply put out your hand, and apologetically announce, "I've forgotten your name." If she wants to make you feel better, she'll say, "Oh, I've forgotten your name too," even if she remembers it! This low-energy start has no place to go but down as you stand around mutually beating yourselves up with a duet of, "I'm so bad with names." "No, I'm much worse." "No, I'm worse that you are—really!" After you commiserate about how dumb you are, you finally reintroduce yourselves, all the while protesting that you'll probably forget each other's names again. Don't ever again say, "I've forgotten your name." Instead, use one of the four techniques above.

. . . .

Don't ever again say "I've forgotten your name."

. . . .

Learn International Names

In this global marketplace, your chances of running into someone who has a name you've never heard before are high. Even a short name can present a challenge. Take the name "Ng," for example. In English, we're tempted to try to pronounce the two consonants together; that's hard to do. For someone from Asia, Ng actually carries the sound of "-ing," just like the most common ending in English for an action—walking, for instance.

Display a friendly curiosity as you learn to pronounce unfamiliar names; set people at ease if they can't pronounce yours. You may decide that you don't want to shorten or change you name just to make it easier for others to learn. Reza from Iran was a little put off when someone at work suggested he just go by "Ray." If you feel that way about your name, then pull out your business card, put on a smile, show the spelling, and lead your contact through the proper pronunciation. "Sri-ni-va-san" chunks it out, saying, "It's got four syllables." In your low-pressure "classroom," people will enjoy the feeling of success when they master your name.

Here are some suggestions for handling the name exchange with other global citizens:

1. Infuse the teaching of your name with energy, clarity, and the assumption that the other person truly wants to learn your name. Helena, who lives in Greece, says, "Hi, I'm Helena, Helena Light. The funny thing about that is that Helena means 'light' in Greek."

2. Approach learning names with warmth and determination. Ask for tips. Ask Mireille about her name. Knowing it's a combination of her parents' first names, Marc and Renée, will help you remember it. You can learn Barbara Rodvani's name when she explains, "Rodvani, think of a van going down a road, Rodvani." Ankur makes it easy for you by saying, "It's like keep the music playing—encore." Don't shy away from learning names that are unfamiliar to your ear. Ask questions in an interested tone of voice and stick with learning the name until you get it right.

3. When you meet someone, don't make any assumptions about national origin and citizenship. When Ying-Chie, a third-generation U.S. citizen, introduces herself, she is often asked, "Where are you from?" She smiles politely and responds, "San Francisco."

4. Suppose you're lucky enough to meet Academy Award–nominated English movie actor Chiwetel Ejiofor (CHEW-eh-tel EDGE-ee-oh-for). Wouldn't you like to know how to say his name? If you know in advance how to spell the names of people you are about to meet, check the pronunciation online by typing into your search engine "how to say that name." Or, type into Google, "how to pronounce (name)." See what pops up.

Let go of the worry that you are going to offend someone, or that they are going to offend you. We're all learning. Showing curiosity, interest, and enthusiasm will go a long way toward creating relationships across the globe.

Join Groups Comfortably

In any room full of people, most people will be talking in groups. You can certainly look around to find someone who is not attached to a group and strike up a conversation with that person. Barbara says, "When I feel nervous about joining a group, I form my own. I look for someone standing alone, and I think the person is so glad I took the initiative."

Or you can join a group. In our workshops, people ask, "How can I break into a group?" We tease them a bit. "Well, first, you find a big sledgehammer. . . ." We choose not to use the phrase "break into a group." When you join a group, think of it as being incomplete until you showed up! This reframing is another addition to your upbeat mindset about connecting in the Network-Oriented Workplace.

To join in the group, signal that you're committed to becoming part of the conversation. You might gently but firmly touch the arm of one person. Almost always, the circle will open up to allow you to enter. Don't be tentative; show commitment by making eye contact with the person who is speaking or smiling at one of the listeners. Take a few seconds to listen. Start participating any time you feel tuned in to what's going on. When the conversation slows, turn to a person next to you and introduce yourself. Often, others in the group will follow suit. If people in the group seem to be acquainted, ask, "How do you all know each other?" as a way to prompt introductions.

If someone quickly introduces everyone in the group to you, don't despair. Simply go back to each individual later and say, "Sam introduced us earlier. I'm Sacha, Sacha Vironski. Tell me your name again."

* *

If joining a group of people who are talking is uncomfortable, analyze why.

* *

If joining a group is uncomfortable for you, analyze why. Are you remembering high school, with its cliques, in-groups, and out-groups? Most of us have vivid memories of feeling excluded at one time or another. Even as grownups, it's easy to still carry around some of that teen trauma. When you bring those feelings out into the light of day and examine them, they usually seem quite ridiculous and based on leftover adolescent angst:

"They don't think I'm cool enough."

"They're probably talking about me."

"They don't want me to be a part of their group."

"They will laugh at me or look the other way."

Sounds pretty silly to hang on to those assumptions now, doesn't it? So, as part of your networker identity, choose to believe that you're on equal ground with others and that others are as eager to get to know you as you are to know them. As you learned in Chapter 1, these mental decisions you make greatly affect your body language and the vibes you give off. Choose to act confident; others are much more likely to see you as approachable and experience you as easy to talk with.

When a new person joins your group, smile, nod, and make eye contact. When the person who is talking finishes his point, fill the newcomer in. Say, "Michio was just telling us about his new project." Then look back at Michio, so he can continue.

There are two kinds of groups *not* to join. One is a group that's working on something. Imagine that Sally, Hank, and Joe were supposed to have planned the meeting that's going to start in four minutes. Joe's email was down, so they need to plan it now. They're busy, and you can see it in their body language and harried look—not a good group to join.

The other group to avoid is made up of people who know each other so well and are having such fun that you'd feel out of place. Imagine that Lou, Henry, and Leia all went to the same college and have just run into each other for the first time since graduation. There's hugging, laughter, and sometimes more touching than in most groups. They're talking all at once. You might notice there's a lot of hand and arm movement. Their voices may be higher or lower than in most groups. This is a good group to avoid because you don't share that college bond. If you were hoping to speak to Henry, come back later, when he'll be more receptive. Trust your powers of observation to find a group that's just right for you.

If you enter a conversation that seems too personal, or if you join one where the topic doesn't suit you, you can leave comfortably. If the conversation is too personal, say, "Looks like I've interrupted something. I'll talk with you later." Or, "Oh, excuse me. Jerry, let me catch a word with you before you go." Or, if the topic is something you're not interested in say, "Hey, I'll talk with you later. It looks like you're really getting into this topic."

11 Tips for Avoiding Awkward Moments

Whether you are at a networking event, or hosting a client at dinner, or chatting with coworkers before a meeting begins, keep these tips in mind. If you do, your connections and conversations will be ones that build trust.

Tip #1: Be polite and positive. Don't ask, "Has your boss finally stopped snapping at everyone?" Don't ask, "Are profits in your division still taking a dive?" Or, "Is your wife still looking for a job?" When people are going through rough times, let them bring up the topic when and where they want to. The Stage of Trust you've reached together will guide you in knowing what's appropriate.

Tip #2: Put some enthusiasm into your conversations. There's nothing more deadly than talking with someone whose energy is low and who has nothing to give. One way to energize a lifeless conversation is to notice or appreciate something about the other person. "You sure were taking lots of notes as the speaker talked. What did you like about what she said?" Or, "The new format you came up with for our Employee Resource Group meetings is ingenious."

Tip #3: When it's been a while, choose your opener carefully. Don't berate yourself for not remembering all the details about a person you talk with only occasionally. Avoid inadvertently putting your foot in your mouth when you begin a conversation with someone you haven't talked with recently. Assume that the person's life has changed. It probably has. Instead of asking, "How's your wife?" ("We're divorced.") Or, "How's your job?" ("I was laid off."), ask more general questions like, "How's your year been?" Or say, "We haven't talked in a while. Catch me up on what's new with you." That allows the other person to reveal as much, or as little, as he wishes.

Tip #4: Go for the relationship, not the contract. When you meet casually—or even at a networking event—and the conversation moves to "let's do some business," set up a convenient time to call or place to meet to complete the transaction. Then, as you continue to talk in the casual meeting, build your relationship with your contact. If you swap stories about parenting, or kayaking, or doing business in India, you'll develop more trust. He'll be more likely to think of you when he needs your services than if you spend most of the conversation aggressively pushing for his business.

Tip #5: Make your Agenda clear when doing business with friends. Relationships that bounce back and forth from friendship to business can be tricky, no doubt about it. To keep the boundaries clear and avoid abusing a friend's trust, be scrupulously honest about your intentions.

Nedra and Alejandro had known each other for 15 years. Alejandro's job was eliminated, and he went into business for himself. Nedra, the marketing director for a communications firm, visited with Alejandro at several professional meetings during the year. Then Alejandro called Nedra and set up a lunch meeting, saying, "I'd love to hear more about that solar cottage you said you're building off the grid. I also want to tell you about some seminars I just finished doing for employees at another company. I think your organization might find them useful." Alejandro made his Agenda clear as he was issuing the invitation. Their lunch conversation ranged from personal items to the seminar series. Nedra asked for additional information about the seminars and appreciated that he was up front about wanting to sell to her.

Tip #6: Decide what to share and what to keep private. Whether face to face or online, be clear about what you want to share with others. Marina, an attorney with a mid-sized firm, is careful about bringing her passion for doing stand-up comedy into business conversations because she's afraid it might confuse her identity or give the wrong impression as she establishes her expertise as a lawyer. On the other hand, even though adoption law isn't her specialty, she has two adopted children, so she freely shares her personal story and then refers prospective parents to an attorney with many years of experience in that field.

Tip #7: Take yourself seriously. It will make talking with you much easier. You create an awkward moment for others if you say, "I'm just an intern." Or, "I'm just a secretary." Don't put yourself down. You discourage conversation if you say things like, "I'm no good at that." If you think you're a whole lot less experienced than others you're talking with, then be sure you're prepared with other topics to talk about that do show your expertise.

Tip #8: Avoid secret language. Some people throw around jargon and acronyms as a way to impress others. Don't do it. If you say, "I'm the EXO for the DDG at the IDB," you'll stop the conversation cold. When talking with people, especially if they are outside your company and occupation, be sure you translate any specialized language into terms that anyone can understand.

Tip #9: Don't ask for free advice. If you speak with someone who has an area of expertise he usually gets paid for, don't try to get free advice. It's one thing to talk with a doctor about those commercials with the voices in the background reciting all of the awful side effects of drugs. It's another thing to drag out your symptoms and ask for a diagnosis. Sometimes the line is unclear. If you feel you might be stepping over it, ask, "Do I need to make an appointment?"

Tip #10: When you don't know what else to say, just say "Hi!" National Public Radio did a survey asking, "What's the best way to start a conversation?" The result? Just say, "Hi!" That's it—just "Hi!" There's nothing hard to remember about that.

But a word of advice: it's not the low-energy "Hi" that says, "I'm just saying this to be polite, and I hope you won't take this as a signal that we have to talk." It's not the kind of "Hi" that says, "I don't really want to be here and I've really got better things to do than talk to you, but 'Hi,' anyhow."

It's a friendly "Hi!" One that flashes this message in neon lights: "I feel great about meeting you, and I'm eager to talk." It's a "Hi!" that says, "I'm glad I'm here, and I'm looking forward to getting to know you." It's inviting and energizing at the same time because it signals that you're a person who is committed to showing up and reaching out. It's relaxing because it signals that you're a person who can take care of herself in a conversation. Practice the two kinds of "Hi!" Feel the difference between the two. Make sure that your tone of voice and body language convey your infectious energy.

Tip #11: Exile the electronics. Put away that smartphone and give your full attention to the person in front of you. Even though you might see others trying to "two-track" conversations, saying hello while checking that last email, don't do it. It's rude. There's no excuse for it. If you must check a message, excuse yourself, find a private place, take care of your electronic business, and then come back to your face-to-face conversations, fully present. If you're out to dinner with friends or business colleagues you might even want to propose the "phone stack" game. Everyone agrees to put his or her cell phone in the middle of the table. The first person to reach for his has to pick up the tab for the whole group.

Helping Others Connect

"The association I work for is unusual in that everyone on the staff goes to the annual convention—all 78 of us! Every day the convention floor is a whirlwind of activity and each of us has many different responsibilities. But Colleen, our Executive Director and CEO, says, 'Your number-one job is to help the attendees feel connected and comfortable.'

"Although Colleen is a natural when it comes to networking, she realized that many of us on her staff needed some coaching to be able to set a warm, welcoming tone for our 8,400 attendees. I was relieved because a lot of times I don't feel connected and comfortable myself, so how can I help others?

"Colleen scheduled a skills training course for us, so we could learn how to handle the most common situations: introducing people, teaching and remembering names, involving people who seem unconnected, getting in and out of those little clumps of people who are talking with each other, and ending conversations graciously.

"I asked the trainer about an awkward situation at last year's conference. I was talking with Person A. She and I had worked on a committee together a couple of years ago. Person B came up and I knew I should introduce them to each other, but in the press of the moment, I didn't recall Person A's name! We role-played the situation and came up with three different ways to handle that situation. Whew!"

End with the Future in Mind

If someone asked you, "What's the most difficult moment in networking?" would you say, "Ending the conversation?" Many people do. Introductions and meeting people are stressful, they'll tell you, and even though the ritual doesn't work very well, everyone plays along: You shake hands and exchange names. But there is no protocol for ending conversations—unless you use the tired, old line, "I'm going to freshen my drink." Exiting can often seem awkward.

LISTEN FOR THE BELL

At networking events and at many business social gatherings, such as cocktail parties or receptions, there's a bell that goes off in people's minds after a conversation has been going on for five or ten minutes. Notice the bell in your head—your intuitive sense telling you it's time to say goodbye and move on.

You may be eager to talk with quite a few different people. Your conversation partner might like to also. Even the best conversations have to end. Assume you'll see this person in the future, and that you'll continue your conversation. Choose the attitude that says, "I'm just beginning this relationship. I'm excited to see what develops." To prepare for your future conversation with this person, make your closing a *conscious* one. Honesty is rare in the final moments of a conversation, but that's what works best.

MAKE A CONSCIOUS CLOSING

Here are seven ways to leave a conversation gracefully and professionally with your own integrity—and your contact's—intact. Read them carefully and make them a part of your repertoire. You won't use all of them at any one time, but by themselves and in combinations, they will make leaving more comfortable—and help you reap many benefits.

1. *Center on your Agenda.* Your Agenda will serve you well as you make conscious closings. Saying, "I want . . . , I must . . . , I need . . ." eliminates the feeling that you are abandoning your conversation partner. Shift the attention to where you are going and the purpose that is motivating you.

Here's what closing a conversation by referring to your Agenda might sound like:

> "I've promised to welcome newcomers, so I'm going to say so long for now."

> "I need to see two more people about board business before I leave tonight. See you soon, I hope."

> "I must speak to the membership chairman before he leaves. Catch you later."

> "I want to see if there are any other engineers (or people from my industry, or people from Washington) here today. Nice talking with you."

2. *Ask your contact for an introduction.* To change conversation partners, let your current partner know the kinds of people you'd like to meet. Say:

> "I want to find other people who are telecommuting. Do you know anyone who is?"

> "Do you know anyone here who is involved with management training?"

> "I'm going to the annual meeting in Dubai next month. Do you know anyone who went last year?"

> "My company is expanding its office design services. Do you know of anyone who is thinking about moving to a new office this year?"

3. *Invite your contact to do something with you.* If you feel uncomfortable ending a conversation and walking away from someone, invite that person to go with you. Your invitation might sound like this:

> "Let's see if we can find the registration booth."

> "Want to get a drink? I'm thirsty." (An aside: this is *sooooo* much better than "Let me go freshen my drink.")

> "I want to ask the speaker a question. Want to come with me?"

4. *Introduce your contact to others.* People will appreciate that you help them meet others. Do you see someone you want to introduce your conversation partner to? Don't think of this as a way to get rid of somebody. Add, "I'm a great connector" to your networker identity. Ask yourself, "Who do I know here that my contact might like to meet?" Say, "Lenora, you mentioned you're going to Vancouver next month. I want to introduce you to Sam. He grew up there and could tell you all about the sights." Or, "Tom, I'd like to introduce you to Bill. He's also new to the firm."

5. *Play Concentration.* Remember that kid's game where you lay all the cards face down on the table? You turn over a three of hearts, but you can't have it until you find a match. Your challenge is to remember, after several turns, where that three of hearts is.

You can play Concentration in a room full of people, too. To get started, listen very closely to what Maria has to say and then introduce her to someone else she might like to meet. And your reason can be anything they have in common: "Oh, you grew up in Chicago. Let me introduce you to Jim—that's his home town, too!" Or, "Oh, you have twins? Let me introduce you to Susan. She does too." You might stay with that conversation or you might excuse yourself once the others get going. But they know that you have listened to them. And people do appreciate being introduced to others around the room.

Suppose you meet Marjorie, an interior designer, who specializes in helping seniors downsize and move to smaller quarters. A few minutes later, you talk with Cynthia, who says she's writing a book titled *Moving Mother.* You think to yourself, "I must introduce Cynthia to Marjorie. What a match!" You go out of your way to bring them together. Whether you stay with that conversation or not, they will remember you as resourceful and generous.

6. *Sum up and appreciate.* One of the most memorable ways to close a conversation is to sum up what happened and then show appreciation for what your contact gave you. To do that, shake hands and acknowledge the conversation and its importance to you. You could even acknowledge the importance in your life of the relationship you have with your contact that, perhaps, goes way beyond this encounter. Find a specific quality in the other person or a specific moment in the conversation that you can genuinely express appreciation for:

"If the other members of AQS are as enthusiastic as you are, I'm going to be very glad I joined."

"Wonderful to see you and get your advice about exhibiting at the trade show."

"I'm so glad to know more about your department."

"Thanks for telling me about your new marketing tactics and the vendor you use. I'll check him out."

7. *Explain the next steps.* Finally, say what you will do next, or what you would like for your contact to do next, to continue the relationship. That reassures your contact that instead of just melting into the crowd, you intend to take action. Promising to follow through signals interest and builds trust. Let your sincerity shine through. Look the person in the eye. Ask her for her card, so you'll have the necessary information to stay in touch. Jot a note to yourself on the back of the card or in your phone while you are still with the person or soon after you part. Say what you will do or what the next step in your relationship will be:

"I'm going to send you that article we talked about."

"This idea really jelled for me when you explained it. I'd like to hear more when we get together next week."

"I'll ask Jackson to call you right away."

"I'll see you at the next meeting."

"So we've decided to meet for lunch next week. I'm so glad."

"Let's talk more about that idea after the holidays."

Or ask your contact to follow up:

"Give me a call next week, and we'll set up a time to talk about working in Thailand. It was the highlight of my year, and I'd love to tell you what I learned before you go there."

Remember watching a wonderful miniseries? Remember the good feelings of expectation you had when you saw the words, "To be continued . . ." on the TV screen? That's how you want to leave your contact, with those words hanging in the air, setting the stage for the next episode in your relationship.

Make these new relationship rituals part of your repertoire. Social skills pave the way for trust to grow.

The Likeability Link

Suppose you want to choose someone to work with you on a project. And suppose that your first choice, someone who is both competent and likeable, isn't available. Who would you choose next? Someone who's competent but not likeable, or someone who's likeable but not competent?

According to a study by Tiziana Casciaro and Miguel Sousa Lobo called, "Competent Jerks, Lovable Fools, and the Formation of Social Networks," most people *say* they would choose someone who's competent but not likeable. But when the researchers looked at whom people *actually* chose, they were surprised. Likeability trumped competence. That's right, in this study, reported in the June 2005 *Harvard Business Review*, most people chose to work with people they experienced as likeable, rather than with people they viewed as the most competent. In the Network-Oriented Workplace, people come together voluntarily, creating their own informal networks. Collaboration and the resulting value creation happen when people trust each other. And likeable people are just easier to trust.

You can learn and use all the rituals we've looked at for introductions, and endings, but if you're not likeable, it won't matter. So let's explore three questions:

1. What is likeability?

2. Does likeability really matter?

3. Can likeability be learned?

WHAT IS LIKEABILITY?

When Lockheed Martin named Marilyn A. Hewson as the new CEO in 2012, Robert J. Stevens, the outgoing chief executive, said, "She is a genuinely likeable person who understands people and connects at an individual level." What did Stevens mean?

Many people have tried to come up with a good definition. Tim Sanders in his book, *The Likeability Factor*, says likeability depends on being friendly, having empathy for the feelings of others, and being able to connect with what other people want and need. Some experts say you can be successful without being likeable. Others disagree, saying you can't get to the top without the help of other people and that people only help people they like. Guy Kawasaki, author of *Enchantment: The Art of Changing Hearts, Minds, and Action*, claims that "you'll know you're likeable when you can communicate freely, casually, and comfortably with people."

In their book *The Axis of Influence*, Michael Lovas and Pam Holloway outline four principles of likeability. We like people who:

1. Are familiar to us in some way (familiarity).

2. Are similar to us in some way (similarity).

3. Are genuinely interested in our concerns and values (interest).

4. Are easy to like in return (trustworthy, positive, nonjudgmental, and real).

The bottom line is that being likeable draws people toward you. Familiarity creates more liking. When two people who like each other connect and converse, good things happen. Trust grows. New networks spring up. New ideas blossom. New value is created.

Casciaro and Lobo write that if someone is disliked, others don't care if he's competent. They won't want to work with him. "By contrast, if someone is likeable, his colleagues will seek out every little bit of competence he has to offer." It was always the case that "a little extra likeability goes a longer way than a little extra competency in making someone desirable to work with."

DOES LIKEABILITY REALLY MATTER?

Take a look at some additional research and decide for yourself.

• "Popular workers were seen as trustworthy, motivated, serious, decisive, and hardworking, and were recommended for fast-track promotion and generous pay increases. Their less-liked colleagues were perceived as arrogant, conniving, and manipulative. Pay raises and promotions were ruled out regardless of their academic background or professional qualifications," says Melinda Tamkins, consultant and executive coach at Ninth House.

• In polls prior to every presidential election since 1960, only one of three factors is a reliable and consistent predictor of who will win. Issues? No. Party affiliation? No. Likeability? Yes. That research was done by Gallup, Inc.

• In interviews with almost 7000 decision makers, "only 17 percent said they could remember more than one time when they had the option not to buy and still went ahead and bought from a salesperson they didn't like," reports Mitch Anthony, author of *Selling with Emotional Intelligence*.

CAN LIKEABILITY BE LEARNED?

Likeability is made up of behaviors—and behaviors can be learned. As Pam Holloway, coauthor of *The Axis of Influence*, says, "Likeability is not magic. It's not luck. It's not a gift inherited by only a few." Just as you add to your competence by learning new skills and taking in knowledge, you also can learn behaviors that will increase the likelihood of likeability. People will say things about you like, "I really like Gita. Let's see if she'll work with us." Or, "Jeff is one of my favorite people. You'll love working with him."

Likeable behaviors send positive messages. When you go out of your way to see Maria, you're saying, "I enjoy you." When you ask Majid's opinion, you're saying, "I respect you." When you save an article about something you know Arnie is interested in, you're

t's these kinds of behaviors that help you mo
Trust that are described in Chapter 4.

. . . .

...eable behaviors send positive messages.

. . . .

When we asked our clients, "Tell us what behaviors make the people you work with likeable," they talked about actions like the ones in the list below. As you read through them, put a checkmark next to the ones you'd be comfortable doing as you build relationships:

_____ **1.** Smile at or wave to someone from across the room.

_____ **2.** Offer to bring someone a cup of coffee.

_____ **3.** Introduce a new colleague to several people.

_____ **4.** Offer to give a coworker a ride to the meeting.

_____ **5.** Say "Thanks for your help" by sending a funny card.

_____ **6.** Nod your head "yes" when someone says something you agree with.

_____ **7.** Stop what you're doing and give someone your full attention.

_____ **8.** Notice that someone needs a seat and get another chair or move over to make room.

_____ **9.** Invite someone to move to a quieter part of the room, so you can hear each other better.

_____ **10.** Remember that someone likes oranges and save one for him.

_____ **11.** Say, "I really enjoy talking with you."

_____ **12.** Show joy on your face when someone you like comes into the room.

_____ **13.** Respond quickly when someone leaves you a messa

_____ **14.** Put your phone away when you're in a face-to-face conve sation.

_____ **15.** Change your plans, so you can talk together longer.

_____ **16.** Ask a thought-provoking question.

_____ **17.** Bring someone a small or silly gift that has meaning to the two of you.

_____ **18.** Find the humor in the situation when someone makes a mistake.

_____ **19.** Keep good eye contact when talking with someone.

_____ **20.** Invite the other person to go first when you're in line together.

Choose several behaviors that you marked and look for times when you can comfortably use them to signal that you like someone. Hopefully, you've put a checkmark next to most of the suggestions listed above.

Robert Cialdini, an author and expert in the field of influence and persuasion, notes that finding something to like in the other person often means they will return that positive regard. Guy Kawasaki, author, investor, and business advisor, says, "If you don't like people, people won't like you."

To be successful in the collaborative workplace, you want to be included in other people's networks and you want them to say "yes" when you invite them to participate in yours. Increasing your social acumen will make the right things happen.

6

....

Deepen Interactions

Strategic Connections: Support Women's Leadership

At one of the world's leading e-commerce companies, the Senior VP of Diversity and Inclusion wanted to make a statement: "We value women leaders, and we support the problem-solving networks you are building." The Senior VP decided that even though it would mean a huge investment of time and money, it would be worth it to bring them all together, face to face. The planning took many months. Finally, the 200 top-level women from all over the globe were invited to a conference at the company headquarters in California.

"We didn't want the attendees sitting in meetings looking at PowerPoint presentations; we wanted them to talk to each other, share experiences, problem solve, and build the kinds relationships they could call on long after the conference was over," said the organizer. "And we wanted the message about our support for their work and their careers to trickle down to the grassroots women's networks that were forming in many locations."

LOOK BACK AT the Big Picture diagram in the Preface. You'll see that the step between connecting and collaborating is conversing. There are five separate, yet interconnected, conversation skills. Mastering these skills will make developing relationships easier and more comfortable. Most people haven't given much thought to what goes into having good conversations. When you master the skills in Competency 6, you'll learn how to enrich your interactions as you:

- *Talk:* Get into dialogues that build and sustain relationships.

- *Question:* Ask questions that make people stop and think.

- *Listen:* Pay attention to the three things that are important.

- *Give:* Offer resources and ideas that signal you want to connect and collaborate.

- *Reconnect:* Follow through and stay in touch in ways that build trust.

Why People Don't Talk

Mark was at company headquarters for a two-day training workshop. Both days he arrived at the classroom about 15 minutes early. Sitting down at the back of the room, he took out his smartphone to catch up on his email.

So why wasn't Mark talking with his colleagues? There are many possible answers. A couple of them reflect his lack of skill in this very important competency; several more reflect his undeveloped networker identity.

- He wasn't aware that those 15 minutes were a ChoicePoint.

- He considered those minutes before class personal time, not work time, not networking time. In his mind, he was "off duty."

- He was drawn to the apparent immediacy of the electronic communication with its pinging alerts.

- He had no Agenda—nothing he had decided that he wanted to talk about—no "mission."

- He felt uncertain and uncomfortable because some others in the class were not only strangers from other departments and divisions, but also from other cultures.

- He preferred an electronic mode of communicating because it allowed him to respond when and how he liked and made few demands on him emotionally.

- He was indifferent because he thought conversation was just "small talk," and he didn't realize how valuable it could be.

- He didn't have much practice or any training in face-to-face communication.

- He didn't link talking to getting his job done or contributing to his organization.

What about you? Have you, like Mark, opted out of opportunities for conversation? Once you realize that there are specific and learnable skills involved and that conversation is fundamental to building trust-based relationships, you'll be able and eager to make the most of a lot of those serendipitous opportunities. You can make interacting more purposeful and rewarding. You'll find that all of the conversation skills will help you enjoy, explore, and exchange.

Talk: Get into Dialogues That Build and Sustain Relationships

Use these tips to help you reach out to people and energize those interactions.

Organize some openers. Do your brain a favor and, before you go to an event, think of several openers. What could you say to start a conversation with the person sitting next to you at a workshop? With someone at an all-hands meeting? With a potential client? Here are some possibilities: "The title of this workshop really grabbed my attention. Is your agency finding recruiting a challenge, too?" Or, "Are you a new employee like me or a long-timer?" Or, "I'm part of the downtown revitalization project team. Have you read about it in the newspaper?"

Add something new. Conversations need your unique contributions. When Georgina and her coworkers chatted before their online meeting got started, she said, "This is my hundredth day with the company!" That sparked a lively exchange in which people said how long they'd been with the company. Similarly, when Al and Sam were at lunch, Al was ready to field the typical questions like "How are you?" and "What's new?" Rather than responding with "Not bad" and "Not much," Al offered that he was about to go to a conference. Sam said he'd arrange for Al to meet with an old friend of his who would also be attending. Who knows what opportunities might have been lost if Al had never mentioned the upcoming conference? When you speak up and add something new, you go from the superficial to the specific. Content counts. Be sure you have your Agenda in mind, so you can add topics you care about to the conversation.

· ·

To go from the superficial to the specific, speak up.

· ·

Appreciate other people. When was the last time someone told you something they appreciated about you, for no reason, out of the blue? Maybe you were a little embarrassed, but wasn't it wonderful? Didn't it brighten your day and give you a special connection to that person? Your willingness to give appreciation to other people is a sign of your confidence and strength. As your capacity for gratitude grows, your ability to give grows. No phony baloney stuff here, please. Just ask yourself from time to time, when you're with people, "What do I appreciate about this person? What would feel good to acknowledge about this person?" Fran said to Hatsumi, "I really admire your skill in turning around disgruntled customers. You're incredible!" Bill told his son's soccer coach, "I think you ought to know that at our house, you are the most frequently quoted expert on almost everything. Several times a day Louis says, 'Coach Baxter says . . .' or 'Coach Baxter wants me to. . . .'"

Play a little. Business conversations can feel heavy, stale, and boring if you can't laugh a little together. Marquette University professor Father John Naus, once said, "We rarely succeed at anything unless we have fun doing it." How true. We're not talking about having a joke for every occasion, but rather seeing the light side, relaxing for a moment in the midst of serious business talk, and laughing together to create a feeling of camaraderie. Phil ran into some coworkers going home on the commuter train the day he was promoted. The car was crowded, so Phil was hanging on to the strap. Then, Jake scooted over on the seat and said, "Here, Phil, sit down. If they can make room for you at the top, we sure can make room for you at the bottom."

. . . .

Lighten up, laugh a little.

. . . .

Look for differences. It's fun to find out that you and your contact both grew up in Texas, or both have MBAs, but don't shy away from exploring all the wonderful, wacky ways you're different, too. You love anything that has to do with numbers, finance, budgets; she majored in music and loves performing. You grew up in "Smalltown, USA"; he grew up in Italy. Dive into those differences in order to learn something and gain new perspectives. Say, "Tell me about that. What was it like to grow up in Naples?" Networks that are diverse in age, gender, culture, function, geography, rank, and any other category expand your thinking and present you with unexpected and out-of-the-ordinary ideas and resources.

Engage with energy. Ever noticed how hard it is to talk with someone who refuses to get excited about anything, someone who, no matter what topic comes up, responds, "Whatever"? Don't be that person. Think of it like this: There's an invisible string going from you to each person you meet. You can decide to make that string zing with energy or let it lie there, limp and lifeless. One way to show your energy and enthusiasm is with your facial expressions. If you say, "I'm so glad to meet you," but your face doesn't match your words, guess which people will believe? Another way is with your voice. Most people have a five-note tonal range. If you never get out of those five notes, your voice is a monotone and you risk coming across as bored and boring. When Marcia said, "My boss asked me if I would give the presentation," she emphasized one word that gave her feelings away. Colleagues could tell that Marcia was surprised and delighted because her voice went up on the word "me."

. . . .

Don't get stuck in the "same old, same old."

. . . .

Just say no. You might be surprised to find out that saying "no" builds relationships. But if you can't say "no," your "yeses" don't mean a thing. When Bert was asked if he'd lead a task force to look into how to best integrate new hires into the firm, he said, "Thanks for asking, but no. I've been out of school too long. I think Susan or Tim would be much more tuned into the 'school to workplace' transition issues." Can you imagine how trust might have been torpedoed if Bert had said "yes" to a request that was not a good fit?

Take clichés seriously. You ask someone, "How are you?" She replies, "Really busy!" or "Really tired!" You come back with "Me too!" Those are clichés. Instead ask, "What's been keeping you busy?" or "What's the most tiring thing you're dealing with these days?" Clichés are boring, so bore in. Explore them. Or make them more personal. Or make your response unexpected and playful.

● ●

Bored with clichés? Bore in.

● ●

Explore the icebergs. George says, "My life is just crazy right now." That's an iceberg statement. A little is showing, but a lot of what's going on is still submerged. Instead of replying, "Oh, I know what you mean," go deeper. Find out what's hidden. Don't ignore the obvious question waiting to be asked, "What's going on that's crazy?" In one such exchange, Leigh got a surprising answer: "I'm interviewing people for a new job we've created in our department." Leigh's brother applied for the job and was hired. Wasn't she glad she decided to explore!

Notice other people. When you take the time to notice people out loud, it's a sign of respect. You've let the other person know that he or she is visible to you and that you are thinking about him. When you comment on someone's activities, he or she feels recognized and trust grows. Say, "I noticed that you've been traveling much more for your job than you used to. How do you like it?" Or, "You seemed to really enjoy giving that presentation. Have you always felt so comfortable talking to large groups?" Or, "I noticed you made sure everyone got a chance to give their ideas in the meeting. Your facilitation skills create such a good result."

Accept the offer. If you take a workshop on how to do improv, a form of theater with no written dialogue, you'll learn a technique called "accept the offer." That means, if I begin the scene implying that we're on a boat being chased by pirates, you better not come back with the idea that we're on an airplane that's run out of fuel. Just as in an improv scene, your conversation partner will give you ideas about where she'd like the conversation to go. If you ignore the cues, you'll cut off future possibilities. Accept the cues and you'll create more connection and trust. If Marcia says, "Boy, I really could use a vacation," don't come back with, "I'm sick of winter." Instead, pursue the vacation topic. Ask, "Where would you go?"

Raise your expectations. What do you predict will be the value of your next conversation? What you expect is what you'll get. Don't underestimate what can happen. People who persist in calling it "small talk" file it in their minds next to other inconsequential things like "small change" and "small fry." Instead, approach every conversation with this mindset: "I wonder what surprising/amazing/interesting/valuable ideas or resources might come up in this conversation!"

Talking Up the Ladder

If networking with people above you on the organization chart seems daunting, try these strategies.

- *Tell what you do.* Be prepared to tell what you do, *not* with your title, but *with a short example*: "I'm on the team that's looking into strategies for expanding our engagements with current clients. We'll have the report done by the end of the month."

- *Do your homework.* Research the backgrounds of executives on your company website or on LinkedIn. You may find you have a connection that you can mention the next time you run into the person: "I noticed that we both grew up in Chicago."

- *Have some questions in mind.* Here are some ideas. "What was the first job you ever had? What did you learn from that job?" "How did you get into_____ (the healthcare field, serving on nonprofit boards, working abroad)?" "What's the best advice you ever got on being a leader?" "What's your advice for me as I begin _____ (job, project, committee, leadership program)?" Achim Nowak, author of *Infectious: How to Connect Deeply and Unleash the Energetic Leader Within*, gives this advice: "Folks tend to play it safe when speaking to someone who has lots of position power. Don't. Take a risk and ask a surprising question—you will be remembered."

> - *Be ready to give.* For example, Todd said to his VP of Human Resources: "I've just read *To Sell Is Human* by Dan Pink. It's about how to influence others. Have you read it? I think we might use some of the ideas in our business development programs."
>
>   - *Above all, be brave.* When we led a panel of senior women discussing how networking had impacted their careers, every one of them said they had had to overcome their (mostly irrational) fears, especially when talking to those higher up.

Question: Ask Questions That Make People Stop and Think

You'll be known for the questions you ask. Questions show respect. They say, "I'm interested and curious." They reveal your interests and your background. And yes, they even give evidence of your Character and Competence.

Many people seem reluctant to ask questions, let alone to ask good questions that go beyond the standard "Where did you go to school?" or "Where did you grow up?" Somewhere along the way, many of us decided it was safer to adopt an air of indifference, as if we've seen it all, as if nothing surprises us. People tell us, "I don't want to look stupid." Or they say, "I don't want to seem nosy." Or, "Won't people be suspicious if I'm too curious and enthusiastic?" Whatever the reason, it's time to break out of old habits and add a new mantra to your networker identity: Be Seriously Curious.

Be known for the questions you ask.

That's was Matt did. Seeing the fisherman bring his boat up onto the beach, this enthusiastic four-year-old ran up to have a look at the catch. He had dozens of questions: "Why is that one striped, but this one is spotted?" "Does that kind grow any bigger?" "Are all of these fish good to eat?" "Which one is poisonous?" "Do you like to touch them?" "Can they make noise under water?" Matt's curiosity was infectious. Listening to the fisherman talk about his catch, blasé adults on the beach began to gather round the little boat and rekindle their curiosity in life, right along with Matt.

Four-year-olds are curious about everything and don't mind showing it. Connect with some of that four-year-old curiosity. Find a role model. Anyone under the age of five will do. Notice the questions he asks, the sheer joy he has for "finding out." Questions help you uncover a need, a commonality, or a difference you want to explore. You'll move more quickly into the Active Stage of relationship building, a critical Stage in the trust-building process.

Here are a few of our favorite all-purpose questions. Have them ready to use in almost any kind of situation:

- "Catch me up on what you've been doing." This invites the other person to steer the conversation wherever she wishes.

- "What have you been working on lately?" Again, you're showing that you're open to letting the other person to choose what to tell you about—the deck he's building or a project at work.

- "What are you excited about?" Or, "What are you looking forward to?" Both of these questions introduce some emotion into the conversation. That's a great idea, especially when the exchange feels a little flat. Your contact may have to think for a moment before answering, because this is an unusual—and therefore interesting—question. Her answer will give you a peek into her future, so listen for how you can help.

- "Tell me your story." Use your voice, your facial expression, and posture to convey intense, positive interest with this question. Because you can tell a lot about a person by where he starts and what he includes, this is a great getting-to-know-you question.

Conversation Quiz

Read the comments below and look through the possible responses. Which ones do you think would work best to build the relationship?

He says: "I just moved here two months ago."
You say:
A. "I've been here 10 years."
B. "Where did you live before?"
C. "What's it been like getting used to a new city?"

She says: "I'm starting a new company."
You say:
A. "I work for XYZ company."
B. "What's the name of your new company?"
C. "What kinds of people would you like to connect with to help you make a go of it?"

He says: "I just got back from vacation."
You say:
A. "Boy, do I need one of those!"
B. "Where did you go?"
C. "What was your very favorite day like?"

She says: "I found what the speaker said so fascinating."
You say:
A. "Me too."
B. "Do you know her?"
C. "Tell me more about what caught your attention."

As you may have noticed, the "A" responses turn the conversation back to you. The "B" responses elicit a short, factual answer. They show interest and add to your knowledge about your contact. The "C" responses engage the other person, ask for evaluation and opinion, and lead you to commonalities and needs you can respond to.

So choose "A" responses rarely. Choose the "B" responses sometimes. And choose the "C" responses, the ones that have the most potential to create connection, most often.

It's not always possible to have questions preplanned and on the tip of your tongue. Don't just count on serendipity to make the conversation work. Use the ASK formula to come up with questions to make the conversation more purposeful and engaging. The letters in the word ASK will remind you to:

A = Add emotion. Tony sat next to Henri on the plane going from Bangkok to Paris. When Henri said that his company had just been bought, Tony asked, "How did you feel about that?" When Henri said that his last child had left for college and he and his wife were "empty nesters," Tony said, "When our kids grew up, we were elated and sad at the same time. You too?"

S = Seek an opinion. When Jim told Maria about the new software package, Maria asked, "What's the best improvement in this version? What features do you think will need more customization?"

K = Kick it around. When Gloria and Colleen served on the board of directors together, they had many conversations to explore things like, "What are the best ways to increase membership? and What are the biggest challenges our members have that the association can help with?"

ASK questions add emotion, seek an opinion, and invite exploration as you kick an idea around.

You can't always plan specifically what to ask when you want to grow the relationship, but you can deepen the exchange, using the ASK formula ideas.

Listen: Pay Attention to the Three Things That Are Important

Networking doesn't mean doing all the talking. The quiet side of networking is listening. Good conversationalists give others a chance to talk. While talking with several coworkers about the upcoming weekend, Mary noticed Frank hadn't said anything. So Mary turned to Frank and said, "Have you and your family got any plans, Frank?"

Listening isn't just impatiently waiting for your turn to talk.

Listening is not just waiting for your turn to talk. Unfortunately, many people act that way in conversations—impatiently waiting instead of listening. Listening is work. Don't think of it as a passive activity where you just nod every once in a while as you wait for an opportunity to chime in. Listening is active. Give it your undivided attention and focus. You speak at a rate of about 150 words a minute, but you can think more than 500 words a minute. That's one reason you must train yourself to pay attention rather than allow your mind to wander off.

Listening can be a challenge. Networking venues are often noisy. If you're trying to listen to someone in a room where lots of other lively conversations are going on, do what Marsha did. She said to Leonie, "Let's move over there out of the way a bit. I really want to hear what you're saying."

If you call yourself an introvert, listening is probably one of your favorite ways of interacting with people. But be sure to speak up.

Through conversation people get to know your interests and expertise. They learn what to come to you for and what opportunities to send your way. Mentally prepare your Agenda, your list of what you'd like to talk about. If, as an introvert, you feel drained after 30 or 40 minutes of talking with people, take a break. Take a walk down the hall. Or find a private place to stretch, breathe, and gather your thoughts. Recall what's on your Agenda—so you're ready with a topic you're excited about. Then rejoin the group with renewed focus and energy. James told us, "When I need a break, I just take to the stairs and run down four flights, then back up again. Works wonders for clearing my mind!"

LISTEN FOR THREE THINGS

With distractions like noisy rooms and minds that are used to multi-tasking, listening well is a skill that needs to be taken seriously. To sharpen your focus:

1. *Listen for evidence of your contact's Character and Competence.* When Sam tells you about chairing the fund-raising committee for the new wing of the Children's Hospital, what might that mean about his Character and Competence? When Sophia recounts her tale of battling her way through the snowstorm to get to work when lots of her colleagues stayed home, what does that tell you?

2. *Listen for information about the other person's skills and talents.* Mei and Don were on a coffee break at the Department of State. When Don mentioned that he'd just finished designing a short course on giving briefings, Mei asked about it and listened carefully. She knew that her boss was looking for a course on that topic for her team. "*Hmmmm*," she thought, as she noticed his friendly, relaxed style, "Maybe Don would be the guy to teach it for us."

3. *Listen for clues as to what you can give.* Listening generously means hearing not only the words, but also the *needs* of your conversation partner. Once you offer a resource, an idea, or an introduction, your relationship moves to the Active Stage, where you have more chances to demonstrate your Character and Competence and discover your contact's. Sheila and Joan met when they played on the company softball team. During one game, they had time to chat on the sidelines. Sheila mentioned she was going to miss a couple of games because of her business trip to New Zealand. Joan offered to give her an electronic introduction to her sister who lived there and worked for a different division of the company.

Reap the benefits of listening well. You'll find out reasons to follow up. You'll learn something new. You'll develop a reputation as a great connector as you hear good reasons to introduce people to one another. And you'll definitely stand out in a crowd. Giving true attention is so rare that you will make a positive impression. Ken says, "I create an imaginary bubble around me and the person I'm talking with. Six elephants in tutus could dance through the room, and I wouldn't notice." You can bet people remember talking with him.

Listening with a Purpose

"I was new and trying to figure out who's who beyond the organization chart. As part of a team that served internal clients, I needed to get a feel for what the other departments did, and fast.

"I decided it was up to me to find a way to get to know people in all the other departments and get a handle on what they did and how we could help. The cafeteria seemed like the natural place to meet people. So on Monday I went through the food line, gathered my courage, and when I found someone sitting alone, said, 'Hi, I'm Susan. May I join you? I'm new here and don't know many people.'

"Most of the time the person said, 'Sure. Please sit down.' Then I started with, 'Tell me all about what you and your department do—I'm trying to get a good picture of the big picture.' Most people were very glad to be asked, and I learned so much listening to their stories, experiences, and yes, even advice. One person I 'interviewed' was also very new. Another had been there 27 years!

"After using my 'cafeteria method' for a couple of months, I knew a whole lot more about what went on in the organization. Several years later, when I began managing others, I asked each of them to use this method of meeting people and learning about the organization. I said, 'I want you to make sure you know at least one person in each of the departments we serve. That way we can begin to get out in front of what they might need. You'll have someone to go to—a relationship already in place—so if there's ever a problem, we can solve it more easily.'"

Give: Offer Resources and Ideas That Signal You Want to Connect and Collaborate

Whether you're self-employed, working in a small nonprofit, or climbing up the ladder of a large corporation, giving is the heart and soul of your success. Since people collaborate best with people they trust, giving becomes one of the best ways to teach people to have confidence in you.

The act of giving teaches so much about who you are—how well you listen to what people say, the importance you place on the relationship as indicated by the speed of your response, the types of networks you're involved in, and the generosity of your spirit. Your willingness to give reveals what kind of collaborator you'll be. It reveals your view about how the world works.

> *Giving teaches who you are and reveals the kind of collaborator you will be.*

Here's what Donna, a senior sales representative, has to say about giving. "I want to be known as a resource—for lots of things. I like to network on a large scale. Sure it's fun to help my buddies, but much more exciting to think bigger. I don't just give information about my area of expertise, which is frankly rather narrow. I might help a woman I know find a spot on a nonprofit board, for instance, not because I think I'll benefit from doing that, but rather because it feels good, I learn a lot, and I want people to see me as the person to come to when they don't know where to find something. I want to be known as someone who has a wide range of interests and resources and who knows a lot of people."

LOOK FOR "THE GIVE"

In Chapter 2, you learned to make a networking Agenda. Your Give list is a "menu" of resources, ideas, enthusiasms, and expertise, a menu of things you are ready to give away. Have those items on the tip of your tongue, but notice also that people will mention things they need (their Gets) that you can respond to even though you don't have them listed on your Agenda as Gives. So be ready with your Agenda Gives, but also be receptive. Tune into the cues that others give you, and draw on who you are, who you know, and what you know to create a giving connection.

The role of networking in the workplace has changed. In the past, you may have thought of networking as a way to get your job done and advance your career. In today's collaborative environment your networking becomes more other-centered. Giving is a way to impact not only your success, but also the success of others.

Here's how three people used their discretionary energy and their valuable resources to find a Give, help their coworkers, and ultimately impact the quality of work all across the board.

• Marcella met Janelle at the firm's holiday party. Since they worked on different floors and in different departments, they'd never had a chance to talk. Marcella said she was a runner. When Janelle heard that she said, "I'm on the employee fitness task force. We want to do a 5K run in the spring. How about helping with that project?" Marcella said, "I managed a run for charity last fall and learned a lot about planning a successful run. I'd be happy to help. How about including my friend Jon in the planning, too?" And Janelle had the beginnings of her committee.

• Jackson, a seasoned IT guy, wanted to upgrade the intranet he'd just begun to manage for his company. He was especially interested in enticing 20-something employees to use it more. When Jackson mentioned that at lunch with his coworkers, Ben offered to invite several of his young contacts—people he'd gone through orientation with— to serve as an informal focus group. He reserved a private room where people could bring in their lunches, and as they ate, he gathered ideas from the other new hires to give to Jackson.

• Jerry felt great about leading the team while his boss was out on maternity leave—except for one thing. He had no experience running meetings and the very thought of it made him nervous. Jerry told Sheila and Eric about his fears as they carpooled to work. The three had previously worked in the same department and knew each other well. Sheila was a pro at leading meetings. She offered to be Jerry's "shadow consultant," teach him some techniques she used, and cheer him on.

In Chapter 4, you learned to identify the Stage of Trust you're at with each of your contacts. You discovered that at each Stage there are appropriate things to do and say. Likewise, when you give to others, your giving should reflect the Stage of Trust you've reached—and no more. Randy offered to recommend his new neighbor for a job at his company. What was a nice gesture ended up putting Randy's reputation on the line. He hadn't known his neighbor long enough to be assured of his Character and Competence and only learned later that he'd been fired from his previous job for nonperformance.

NEW RESEARCH ON GIVING

Does the idea of helping others put you off? We hear people say things like, "When will I have time to do my own work?" and "What if people take advantage of me?"

Research reported in Adam Grant's book, *Give and Take*, will help you understand how to manage your giving, so that it helps you, others, and your organization. Grant, a professor at The Wharton School of the University of Pennsylvania, advocates being what he calls "otherish"—being willing to help others, but also making sure you achieve what's important to you. Grant identifies three kinds of people in the workplace: Matchers, Takers, and Givers. Matchers want to create a balanced score sheet. You give me something; I give you something back. Takers try to get you to give to them, but put no energy into reciprocating.

The Givers in Grant's studies have the most to teach us about how to operate in the Network-Oriented Workplace. His research shows that some Givers are quite successful, but others are not. So what's the difference? The unsuccessful Givers had no boundaries, got burnt out, and weren't comfortable asking for help themselves. The successful Givers, on the other hand, knew how to set boundaries, express their own needs, and were more likely to find win-win solutions because they were good at empathizing with others.

At the design firm IDEO, they call giving "helping." It's the same idea under another name. In "IDEO's Culture of Helping" in the January/February 2014 issue of the *Harvard Business Review*, the authors say that helpfulness isn't natural; it must be nurtured. Potential helpers might be more used to competing. And people might not ask for help because they don't want to be seen as weak or incompetent. IDEO's CEO, Tim Brown, says, "I believe that the more complex the problem, the more help you need." Leaders prove their commitment to helping by giving and seeking help themselves. Employees get *The Little Book of IDEO* that lists the values of the organization, including

"Make others successful." And the authors point out that trust is what makes a helping, collaborative culture work.

Reconnect: Follow Through and Stay in Touch in Ways That Build Trust

As baseball players and golfers all know, follow-through is the act of carrying a motion to its natural completion. Follow-through ensures that the player achieves maximum force on the ball. It's not a separate act. It's a *natural extension of the initial contact.*

In the same way, *networking Follow-Through* begins with a good first conversation, one in which you listen generously and are seriously curious to find out what's on your conversation partner's Agenda. A meaty conversation will give you ideas about how to follow through. Reconnect based on the other person's Agenda, not yours. So be sure you talk less than 50 percent of the time and learn all you can about your contact.

* *

Follow-Through begins with a good first conversation.

* *

Ideally, you'll suggest another meeting during that first conversation. You might say, "I'd like to talk with you more about that. Can I call you next week to set up a time to get together?" Or say, for example, "I'll give you a call next month, so that we can get together for lunch." The goal is to set up a chain reaction of six to eight encounters. You won't have to initiate every meeting. You know you'll see Tom at the next task force meeting, for example, and you'll reconnect with Clara at the monthly board meeting.

FIGURE OUT REASONS TO RECONNECT

Why *do* you want to get back in touch? Getting clear on that will help you decide how to do it.

1. *Chemistry.* You like the person. You like her energy. You like his sense of humor. She seems easy to talk with. You feel at ease with him. You "click."

2. *Commitment.* You had a rich, Agenda-based conversation that requires some specific next step. You promised to provide a phone number or website or piece of information.

3. *Commonality.* You found you have something in common or uncovered a need that begs to be explored. You can imagine because of what he does (chairs the diversity task force, for instance)/who he knows (people in Seattle where you plan to move next year)/the experiences she's had (worked in London), that it will be mutually beneficial if you make time to talk and get to know each other.

THE FIVE GOALS OF FOLLOW-THROUGH

We've lost track of the number of times participants in our training programs have said, "I met someone once. Now what? I can't just call him up and say, 'Hi! Remember me?'" In Chapter 4, you learned that dormant ties—people you met three months ago or three years ago—can be very valuable. They will often lead you to better solutions and resources than people in your current networks. So set aside any fears you might have, such as, "He won't remember me," or "She's too busy and important."

What are you trying to achieve as you nurture networking relationships? What are your five specific goals? Aim to make use of every interaction to teach your contact:

1. Your name and how to reach you easily

2. Exactly what you do

3. Why she can trust you, whether she works inside or outside your organization

4. What kinds of clients, customers, or job opportunities you are seeking and what you can refer to him

5. What kind of information and opportunities you're looking for

As you reach these goals with your contacts, you'll begin to—and continue to—reap the benefits of networking.

EIGHT REACHBACK STRATEGIES THAT WORK

Be creative in coming up with ReachBack strategies to reconnect intentionally. And what is "ReachBack"? It's a term we invented to emphasize the idea of reaching *back* to dormant relationships—and reaching *out* to the people you are currently working and networking with. Consistent Follow-Through helps you maintain your networking relationships, so that your contacts are ready to help you.

Here are some ideas to get you started:

ReachBack Strategy #1: Set up the "annual" lunch. When you fear it's been too long since you last talked, do what Mack did. He called Tim, whom he hadn't seen in about three years and said, "Hey, it's time for our annual lunch. How about Tuesday?" That lets Tim off the hook—he's probably feeling bad about not keeping up with Mack. Of course, they both know it's been longer than a year, but they have a good laugh and everybody saves face.

ReachBack Strategy #2: Ask for feedback. Ask someone you'd like to reconnect with to review something you've written. Tom writes a short monthly blog for members of the professional association he works for. About a week before his deadline, as a way to stay connected, he sends his blog to a couple of members and to a few coworkers in other departments. He asks for their comments, suggestions, and a reality check. By choosing a different group of "reviewers" each month, he collects new insights, suggestions, and strategies. And the people he asks are honored to have contributed.

ReachBack Strategy #3: Piggyback on other events. Everybody's busy, but isn't it easier to fit in reconnecting if you tack it on to other events? Lorrie met Rhoda at a management training course, delivered in half-day segments, for staff at Georgetown University. A few days before the second session of the course, Lorrie sent Rhoda an email saying, "Looking forward to seeing you at the course. Got time for a quick lunch in the faculty dining room after our session?"

ReachBack Strategy #4: Build a little sweat equity. Did your contact mention a sport? Suggest a round of golf or a bike ride as a way to spend time together. It's a fact that connections and conversations that happen outside of the office often lead to insights about your contact's Character and Competence.

ReachBack Strategy #5: Praise their publicity. Peruse the newspaper watching for publicity about any of your contacts. Clip articles and send them with sticky notes. Or use the Internet to find out what's new. Setting up a Google Alert will bring their news to your inbox. Or respond to a post on Facebook. Giving feedback is a great way to reconnect and stay in touch.

ReachBack Strategy #6: Lend a book. Offer a book or CD you've enjoyed. When Mike met Charles at a Rotary International luncheon, Charles said, "I've been wishing I had a copy of that new book by Malcolm Gladwell." Mike asked for his business card and said, "I have a copy. I'll give you a call and bring it over when I'm near your office tomorrow afternoon." When you stop by, if your contact has time to chat, be ready to ask about projects he or she is working on and ready to tell about your latest projects and challenges.

ReachBack Strategy #7: Have a bunch to lunch. Ask a few people you'd like to know better to lunch. Pick your lunch bunch carefully, so that the benefits of their becoming better acquainted with you and with each other are obvious. Marcella, who owns an advertising agency, reserves the last Friday of every month and invites a mix of clients and potential clients to a catered lunch in her conference room. "They seem to enjoy meeting each other. Often, the stories my current clients tell to my potential clients teach them to best way to use our services."

ReachBack Strategy #8: Find people to thank. Late Friday afternoon, when not much else is going on, look back over your week and find five people to thank. Thank Karishma with a funny card for tutoring you in that new software program. Send Bill an email thanking him for the referral. Send the three people who supported you during your successful job search gift baskets of specialty chocolates. Call Stan to tell him how much you appreciated his advice about how to handle the office move you are managing.

Follow-Through ideas come in all sizes, shapes, and flavors. The more specific they are and the more they relate to the interests and needs of your contact, the better they will be received. Just because you meet Alex once doesn't mean that he wants to be sent your brochure or your newsletter. That's about you, not about him. Given the situation, the contact, and what happened in the first (or most recent) conversation, is it best to stick to electronic communications, or send a note through the mail? Would it be best to look for him at the next meeting or drop by his office? Remember, it's not the amount of time you spend with someone that builds trust. It's the quality of the interaction. Choose face-to-face contact whenever you can.

Through conversation, relationships develop and deepen. Honing all the conversation skills means that you are ready to network—to explore, to enjoy, and to educate. You can add, "I can talk to anybody," to your networker identity.

7

....

Communicate Expertise

Strategic Connections: Tell the Story

A partner at a major design/build firm wanted his engineers, architects, and project managers to talk with prospective clients—until he overheard this conversation. A prospect asked, "How many sports facilities have you done?" A project manager said, "Lots." An engineer said, "Seven—I think."

The partner thought, "They don't know how to talk about our achievements." To test his assumption, he later gave everyone a 10-item quiz that included these questions:

- *Who are three corporate clients the firm has enjoyed repeat business within the last 10 years?*

- *How many sports facilities has the firm completed since entering that market five years ago?*

- *The firm led a design team to protect and encase documents that are more than 225 years old. What were the documents and where are they housed?*

> *His staff members came up with the right answers to only 30 percent of the questions. One architect asked, "How would we ever get this information?"*

HOW CAN YOU teach contacts to trust you? You can show them or you can tell them. You show them when they see you in action. You tell them when you talk about yourself, your team, or your company. Competency 6 covers how to tell people about yourself—without bragging. In conversation, you'll find many opportunities for storytelling that makes your expertise come alive and makes you—and your organization—memorable. One prime time occurs when someone asks you, "What do you do?" Another time comes when you hear another question, "What's new?"

Answering "What Do You Do?"

When answering the "What do you do?" question, you teach people not only about your job, but also about your Character and Competence. But, as with Name Exchange, all too often the rituals we have learned so well, and toss off so effortlessly, get in the way of building relationships and finding out more about each other. Whether you're answering the "What do you do?" question from colleagues at work or from contacts outside, your answer can energize and steer the conversation—or fall flat.

WHY THE USUAL ANSWERS DON'T WORK

Do you respond to that oft-asked question with your *occupation*? If you say, "I'm an attorney," that's Cement. The response falls like a dead weight—a block of cement—at the other person's feet. There may be 37 other attorneys in the room, so you just missed the chance to make yourself unique. And your conversation partner is likely to say: "Oh . . . nice." (Yep, that's the number-one comeback when people hear what you do.)

Do you respond with your *title*? If you say, "I'm Technical Outreach Interactive Services Manager with the Northeast Division of Tri-State Corporate Systems, a division of System Information International, Inc.," that's Fog. Giving a title—especially a long, complicated, jargon-filled one—leaves your conversation partner surrounded by a thick cloud of words. And your partner will probably come back with, "Oh . . . nice."

Do you respond with your *industry*? If you say, "I'm in real estate," that's the Blob. That answer puts you right into the middle of the great gray blob of the other 23 people your conversation partner knows who also are in real estate. You've missed your chance to tell about your special talents or your special niche in the real estate industry—what makes you different from all the others. And your conversation partner, not knowing what else to say, probably replies with a polite, "Oh . . . nice."

Do you respond with the name of your *organization*? If you say, "I'm with Disney," that's the Flag. That response wraps you in the flag of the organization. You aren't going to be known for your talents and capabilities if you say that; your only identity will be "one of those Disney people"—a dangerous situation if you ever leave or are laid off. Note that the more prestigious your company is, the more tempting it is to mention it and the more exaggerated the "Ohhhh . . . nice!!" response will be.

> *Don't give your occupation, title, industry, or company.*

What's the problem? These commonplace responses to "What do you do?" aren't conversation builders; they're conversation stoppers.

Your contact may have learned to deal with Cement and the Flag by asking questions: "What kind of law do you practice?" "What do you do at Disney?" But you didn't make it easy for him to talk with you. And you missed the boat when it came to teaching him anything about your capabilities and talents.

MAKE THE RIGHT THINGS HAPPEN

Your conversation partner has a TV screen in her head. Most people do. When you tell her about your work, there are two possibilities.

On the one hand, she may see nothing on the screen—like when your cable is out. That's what people see when you respond to "What do you do?" with Cement, Fog, or the Blob—nothing. On the other hand, if you proudly wave the name of your organization in front of her, the Flag, she may see your company logo or well-known product. This answer may feel good at the moment. There you are, basking in the reflected glory of Mickey Mouse. But you could get so much more. Ask yourself, "What do I want my contact to see on the TV screen in her head? What one thing do I want her to know about me?" When you come up with that, you'll know what to say.

●●●

Put a picture in your listener's mind.

●●●

GIVE IT YOUR BEST

Use our two-sentence formula—the Best/Test—to construct your optimal answer. For your first sentence, your Best, decide on the one thing—of all your many talents and skills—you want people to remember about you. Keep this sentence short, around 15 or fewer words.

For your second sentence, come up with a brief example, a testimonial (the Test) that backs up the talent or skill you highlighted in your first sentence. Use only about 25 words or so to briefly describe how you:

- Saved the day.

- Served the client.

- Solved the problem.

Keep your Best/Test snappy and jargon-free. Aim to be understood by a 10-year-old. Include exciting, colorful, vivid language.

Using the Best/Test formula gives you the best answer.

Keri used to say, "I'm Senior Manager of Utility Plant Construction at Barkus Mangle Harbusson Professional Services Consultants." What a Fog that puts the listener in! Here's Keri's Best/Test answer: "I make sure construction projects stay on time and on budget. At a wind farm going up in Oregon, we've just learned that our community education efforts have succeeded, and residents nearby are now supporting the project." Her listeners now see windmills.

Lisa used to say, "I'm in finance," a Blob answer that told only her industry. Now she focuses on only one aspect of her role as Vice President of Finance at a large healthcare organization for her Best: "I figure out how to come up with the money to build new nursing homes." She updates her Test frequently to provide an ever-changing picture of what she's doing at work: "Right now, I have a team checking out taxes in southern states. I just updated the CEO on our findings and pointed out the impact tax rates can have on our expansion plans." What do you know about Lisa from this short example? Several things. She's a valued member of the executive team. She's proactively providing information that the company needs to make good decisions. Using this kind of Best/Test, Lisa is teaching her contacts about her Character and her Competence—and beginning to build the trust that is necessary to establish an effective networking relationship. That's a major improvement over her original Blob answer.

John used to describe himself as "a marketing consultant," a Cement answer. Now, he tells what he does Best: "I help people get the word out about their products and services." He, too, frequently updates his Test to provide a vivid picture of himself succeeding with clients: "Last week, I wrote a news release that got one of my clients, a CPA, on the front page of Tuesday's business section. Since the article appeared, she's had seven calls from prospective clients!"

What do you know about John from this short example? He writes news releases that get results for clients? He knows the local media and successfully used a news release to get a reporter to write an article? Now, imagine that you run into a CPA who says, "I want to let women entrepreneurs know about my services for small businesses." Wouldn't John's name and expertise pop up in your mental database of contacts? Assuming you've learned enough about his Character and Competence, wouldn't you mention John to this CPA?

Notice that your Best/Test answers provide listeners with two kinds of information—facts and the inferences you can draw from them. Facts are specific and verifiable. John writes news releases. He has a CPA for a client. Inferences are the conclusions that listeners reach based on the facts. John, the listener surmises, must know what kinds of stories the local paper would be interested in, and he must know which reporter to pitch the story to.

> *Best/Test answers provide facts and encourage inferences.*

By the way, we hope you won't call your answer to the "What do you do?" question an "elevator speech" or a "30-second commercial." As we pointed out in Chapter 1, those labels devalue and diminish the very important trust-building and teaching process that goes on in this part of the getting-to-know-you ritual. Your answer is not a commercial; it's a carefully crafted couple of sentences that you use to spark a conversation and begin to teach your contact about your trustworthiness.

BE INTERESTING

If you hear the comment, "Oh . . . nice," when you tell what you do, revise your answer. Aim for the comment, "Tell me more." When people asked Buford "What do you do?" he used to give his title. It was so long that he had to stop and take a breath in the middle: "I'm director of student financial aid in the student affairs division (gasp) at the University of Missouri-Kansas City." And people said, "Oh . . . nice."

Then he came up another way—a much more interesting way—to put it. He said, "I'm in charge of giving away $32 million a year to students. One student we gave a four-year scholarship to just graduated with honors and came by the office say, 'Thanks.'" Did people want to hear more? You bet!

Figure 7–1 offers more examples of vivid ways people tell what they do.

INSTEAD OF:	SAY:
"I'm an organizational development specialist." (Cement)	"I work with teams that are falling apart." (Best) "Last week I led a retreat for 18 people who were so relieved to find out that people from four generations really *can* work together!" (Test)
"I'm with IKEA." (Flag)	"I show people how to create wonderful and livable spaces." (Best) "Right now, I'm working with a team of designers to set up children's rooms to be photographed for our upcoming catalog." (Test)
"I'm in corporate communications." (Blob)	"I make sure employees understand what's going on in the company." (Best) "I'm writing a series of articles that explains the technology behind our new alarm system product." (Test)
"I'm a Global Financial Advisory Specialist with Region Four's Stabilization Outreach Team for Corporate Development." (Fog)	"I work with clients who are buying or selling a business across international borders." (Best) "Last week, we helped a pet food chain buy stores in Denmark." (Test)

FIGURE 7–1. *Transforming Your Answers*

Did you notice the use of "we" in the final example in Figure 7–1? As you devise your Best/Test, you may use "I" or "we," depending on whether you work alone or with a team. Using "we" makes it clear that others were involved. Also, if you're new in your job and don't yet have an example of your own expertise to offer, or if your primary goal is to teach people about your organization, not yourself, you can use a team or company example.

TIPS FOR CRAFTING YOUR BEST BEST/TEST

Here are some things to keep in mind as you come up with several interesting and dynamic Best/Test answers to "What do you do?":

Say the right thing in your Best/Test. Don't choose being sensational or cute over teaching people what you really want them to know about you. A pharmaceutical saleswoman got people's attention when she said, "I sell drugs." But after thinking it over, she decided that was not an image she wanted leave with people. She now says, "I educate doctors about new drugs. Last week I visited a practice of three pediatricians who appreciated understanding more about a new drug for childhood diabetes."

Tell your talent, not your title. Titles tell where you are on the organization chart, not what you do. Instead, put a movie in the other person's mind of you in action, you at your best.

Avoid acronyms and jargon. When the person you're talking with is unfamiliar with your "insider lingo," he will feel put off. If you want to be remembered, translate jargon and simplify your Best/Test.

Resist the ego trip. If you work for a well-known or prestigious group, resist the urge to wrap yourself up in your organization's reputation. If you want to include the name of your company ("I'm with Hallmark" or "I'm at the World Bank") be sure to also include a talent or an example. We guarantee that the name of your organization alone won't start the conversation you want. And worse yet, you just missed the chance to teach someone about your talents and successes.

Ask a question. A variation on the Best/Test is to answer, "What do you do?" with a question. David, a manager with the Federal Reserve, asks, "Has your bank ever put your money in somebody else's account?" Whether the listener replies "yes" or "no," he goes on,

"I'm working with banks nationwide to design a system so that won't ever happen."

Avoid four errors. As you craft your answers, steer clear of the typical mistakes we see people make. *Avoid winging it.* Write out your answers and then get them firmly in mind. If you don't write them, you can't edit them. *Avoid long sentences.* Follow the guidelines about the number of words and aim to keep your answer to two sentences—one for your Best talent and one for your Test. *Avoid extra words that don't really need to be there.* Edit, edit, edit! *Avoid generalities.* Make your example very specific. That's the way to get a picture of you at work in someone else's mind. And be sure to include an example (your Test). Without an example, you haven't proved your point or showed your listener you in action.

Frequently Asked Questions

Here are some questions people ask about the Best/Test formula for answering "What do you do?"

Q: *Should I not give my title and the name of the company I work for?*

A: If you can get into a good conversation, you'll have plenty of opportunities to mention those things later. Just don't make that the only feature in your answer.

Beware! In today's volatile economy, it's a dangerous thing to fall in love with your title and your company. The pleasure you take in introducing yourself with your title and your company affiliation is an indication of your dependency on them for your self-image. You might find yourself out of work. It's far better to teach people about your abilities. For instance, you might want them to know that you are an outstanding trainer who knows how to convey complicated technical information. It's your reputation that will get you your next job, not your current title and company.

Q: *What if I wear several hats?*

A: Everybody does. That's why you need to prepare several different Best/Test responses. Select the right one to use depending on whom you are talking to and what you want him to know about you.

For instance, when we are talking to meeting planners, one of us might say, "I get people talking at conventions." (Best) "I just gave the kickoff keynote on convention networking at the Healthcare Educators annual meeting." (Test)

> *Everybody wears several hats, so everybody needs several Best/Tests.*

When we are talking to people in professional services, one of us might say, "I help lawyers learn what to do and say to find new clients." (Best) "I just finished a four-session series of seminars for attorneys at Arnold & Porter." (Test)

When we're talking to people in the publishing industry, one of us might say, "I wrote *the* book on networking." (Best) "A book club just bought 59,400 copies." (Test)

Q: *Won't I sound like I'm bragging?*

A: Many people in our workshops say, "Oh, I could never say something like that. I'd feel like I was bragging." But are you? See the "What do you do?" question as an invitation to tell what you're excited about, working on, or proud of. A lot of it has to do with your delivery. Your body language and tone of voice can show you're excited about the results you bring for your clients, or the students you serve, or the association members you keep informed.

As the old-time American humorist and storyteller Will Rogers once said, "If you done it, it ain't braggin'." If you're expounding on your new Acura TLX, your private jet, and your house in Fiji, that's bragging. But if you're talking about a project you poured your time, talent, and creativity into, that's not bragging, that's what people want to hear from you. When you're asked what you do, the best way to start a conversation is to be enthusiastic and specific about your accomplishments. How else will people learn what to count on you for, what you're good at, who they should refer to you, and what opportunities they could send your way?

Q: *How will I know when I have a good answer to the question, "What do you do?"*

A: Ask yourself these three questions:

1. Does my answer give a specific, positive picture of me succeeding, me doing what I want to be known for? Does it teach about my Character, my Competence? Does it show what I want to do more of?

2. Does my answer encourage people to say, "Tell me more?" Does it invite questions and conversation without being maddeningly mysterious? The real estate agent who merely says in her Best, "I'm a miracle worker" is being too cagey. She needs to add "for home buyers." Her Test can further verify her claim as she says, "I just found a house for a newly married couple—they both use wheelchairs—at a price they can afford in a neighborhood they love."

3. Do I deliver my answer in an excited, upbeat way, in a tone of voice that expresses my enthusiasm for serving my customers or solving problems, rather than sounding full of myself?

Q: *What should I do if the person I'm talking with gives me Cement (her job type), Fog (her title), or the Blob (her industry)?*

A: Use questions to draw out specific examples, learn about special expertise, or hear about unique projects. Ask:

"What's a typical day like in your work?"

"Tell me about a recent project you've been working on."

"What have you been doing this week?"

"What's your favorite project these days at work?"

Q: *I'm in a technical field. I have a Ph.D. I can't imagine being so folksy—especially when I'm with my peers and everyone is trying to one-up everyone else.*

A: It's okay to use your title or the jargon of your profession if you are speaking to other people in the same specialty. But, be sure to supplement that with a vivid example, so that people have a clear idea of your expertise.

Q: *I hate what I do. I'm just an office manager. It's so boring. I'm trying to change careers. What should I say?*

A: If you don't like what you are doing, don't talk about it. Instead talk about the five percent of your job you do like or what you have done in the past or what you want to do in the future. Mary described the part of her job she liked the most: "I'm an expert scheduler and organizer." (Best) "Last year, when my company relocated, I was in charge of the move. It was so exciting to manage every detail of packing an up-and-running office into thousands of boxes and unpacking it back out again in record time and with a minimum of disruption." (Test) By the way, after using this Best/Test for several months, Mary got a new job as a moving coordinator for a large telecommunications company. She found out about the job in a conversation with someone from the company who responded to her Best/Test with this comment: "Oh, we need you at our company!"

Q: *Won't I need several answers—depending on whom I'm talking to and how well they know my kind of work?*

A: Absolutely! We recommend you have four or five answers you're comfortable giving. One might be for an informal setting such as when you're at the swimming pool with your kids. One might be used internally to teach others in your organization how your work ties to their work or contributes to the bottom line. Another might be used at a conference to guide the conversation toward talking about a particular job challenge. Kim said, "I'm the expert in doing more with less at the agricultural extension office in Wichita. As our budget shrinks, my job grows. Are you facing the same problem?"

Q: *How can I keep my answers to "What do you do?" from sounding stilted or canned? People aren't used to hearing something this long or detailed; they expect a simple job title.*

A: True. A Best/Test answer will set you apart from the crowd—and that's exactly what you want. Say your answer with enthusiasm and as if you know the listener will be interested. Practice it until you know it as well as you know your own name. Your answer shouldn't sound like "resume talk." Keep the language conversational and jargon free so it flows off your tongue easily. Watch for people's reactions and modify your answers until you get the reactions you want.

Getting Conversations Rolling

"I tested the Best/Test idea at a conference when I wanted to connect with the Executive Director of the President's Council on Physical Fitness and Sports," Andy said. "When we met, I said, 'I'm Director of Member Services with the Association of Pedestrian and Bicycle Professions.' I got a blank stare. (I'd already figured out that, when people heard the association's name, they thought I either ran the Tour de France or owned a messenger service!) But later that day, I had a second chance. So, I tried again. (Does it tell you something that the guy from the President's Council had no memory of meeting me earlier in the day?)

"This time, I used my Best/Test answer. I said, 'I work for an association that serves people who want to build more walking and bicycling into their lives and their communities.

We just gave a grant that created 300 more miles of trails in Colorado.' The look of interest on the executive director's face was all I needed to convince me that using the Best/Test formula to answer 'What do you do?' is a much better way to get a conversation off to a good start."

Why Storytelling Works

The skill of storytelling appears in a small way in the short example you give when you answer "What do you do?" Storytelling also plays a bigger role as a trust-building and relationship-building tool. To teach people to trust you, tell stories that reveal your Character and Competence. To build relationships, tell stories that make you—and your experiences—memorable.

Storytelling is essential because most people won't be there when you have your shining moments. If you want them to know how good you are at turning around a bad situation, or what an ingenious solution you came up with, or how you triumphed in a crisis, or how you persisted until you reached your goal, you'll have to tell them. Stories bring your experiences to life. They stick in the mind, so your contacts can repeat them as they talk about you, advocate for you, even recommend you to others. Stories flesh out bare facts and are more convincing. Stories create an emotional connection between you and your listener.

● ●

Stories bring your experiences to life.

● ●

Notice in the following story that Ned's opening question might have been a little sarcastic. Notice how Aaron changed the tone of the conversation without reacting to his manager's comment.

"Have a nice vacation?" asked Ned the day after a big snowstorm had shut down the agency for a day. Aaron said, "Sure did. I decided to tackle a big project—lining up the speakers for next fall's Partnering Conference. Earlier, when I'd tried to call the presenters I had on my list, their phones always went to voicemail. I figured if I was stuck at home, they probably were too. I was right. I talked to all five of them and got commitments from four. They were able to shoot me their bios immediately, so I even got that part of the program written. What a productive day! Then I took my son sledding."

What did Aaron teach about himself? He didn't take the day off. He used the weather situation to his advantage. He made headway on a big project. He made time for his son. His story taught Ned a lot about Aaron's Character and Competence.

With practice, you can identify, write, and tell stories that teach who you are, what to come to you for, what you're good at, what kinds of opportunities to send your way, and what to count on you for. Sometimes you'll tell a story that highlights your successes; sometimes your story might be about your team's or your organization's success.

FIND A STORY

To start the process, ask yourself, "What would I like to teach people about me?" Think of a capability or talent you want others to know about. What point do you want to make? Do you want people to know that you're a stickler for details? That you're creative? That you're compassionate? That you can be tough when the going gets tough? That you know a lot about designing optimal learning environments?

Then look for something that's happened that can serve as an example of one of those things. What event have you been part of that you could turn into a story?

Think about:

- Successes at work and in life.

- Situations that brought out your best.

- Moments of surprise, delight, and outstanding results.

* Times when you faced a challenge or had a problem to solve.

* What others find unique and interesting about you, your job, or your life.

Remember your goals. If, for example, your goal is to teach that your bank has special programs for small businesses, tell a story about a specific small business that used your loan program to expand. If your goal is to teach your contacts that you enjoy pulling together a group of people from diverse backgrounds to come up with creative solutions to marketing problems, tell a story about a time you did just that.

KNOW THE 5-S STORY FORMULA

To create the very best stories, use this formula:

Segue + Situation + SNAFU + Solution + Significance

The Segue is a transition sentence. It signals that you have something to say; it gets you into the story; it bridges from the previous topic; it introduces your topic in a general way. "I've been meaning to tell you. . . ." Or, "Something happened that reminded me of you. . . ." Or, "Remember your experience in Berlin? Well, here's what happened to me there." Or, "We, too, have lots of social media initiatives springing up at our company."

The Situation briefly sets the scene and gives the time, place, and who's involved.

The SNAFU is the challenge or problem you had to solve or what you had to overcome. (SNAFU is military jargon for Situation Normal, All "Fouled" Up.)

The Solution is the turnaround, the dramatic highlight of the story—how you solved the problem. It provides the energy that makes the story memorable and exciting.

The Significance is the positive impact it had on you, or others, or your organization.

As you tell your 5-S story, bring it to life with an energetic tone of voice. Use gestures and animated facial expressions.

SARAH'S STORY

Let's see how using the 5-S formula works. Here's what Sarah put together.

Segue: "I never thought as an engineer I'd spend the day with 100 sixth graders!"

Situation: "Last week was the 'Wow! That's Engineering!' day I coordinated for our Society of Women Engineers' Chapter and Lincoln Labs at Massachusetts Institute of Technology."

SNAFU: "I was worried. What can we possibly do with 100 young girls to get them interested in careers in science and engineering?"

Solution: "Then it hit me—lip gloss! So, our SWE members showed them how engineers came up with the shiny lip goop. We mixed up a batch, and the girls took little pots of it home."

Significance: "One girl said to me as she left, 'I thought engineering was boring. But, this was *sooooo* cool. Thanks!'"

LINDA'S STORY

And Linda? Here's her story:

Segue: "I've been meaning to tell you what happened on the first night of the conference."

Situation: "I was just settling into my hotel room when Dan, my sales manager, called."

SNAFU: "He said that his wife was in labor (two weeks early!), and he wouldn't be able to stay and give his presentation. The organizers had told me when I checked in that 125 people were signed up for his session. He and I had written that presentation together, so I was very familiar with it."

Solution: "All of a sudden I heard myself saying, 'How about if I sub for you? I've got 24 hours to get ready.' Dan said, 'Great. You can do it. Go for it!'"

"For the next three hours I practiced the presentation in front of the mirror in my room. The next morning I checked the room setup, and told the organizers that Dan had had a family emergency, so I'd be filling in."

Significance: "My presentation went off without a hitch. Afterwards almost a third of the audience asked for information about our new product. Dan had told me if only 10 percent did that we'd be doing well, so I was very excited to tell him the news—after he told me about his new baby daughter!"

CAMERON'S STORY

Segue: "I've been working in a tent!"

Situation: "The engineering firm I work for got a contract to do soil analysis around the levees in New Orleans after Hurricane Katrina."

SNAFU: "We knew we had to process about 630 tons of soil from a 350 mile radius in just three weeks."

Solution: "There was no time to find a good facility, so we set up our soils testing laboratory in a parking lot in a huge tent I rented from a wedding supply company."

Significance: "There were two things that made me want to finish that project in record time. One was that it was 99 degrees in that tent. Believe me—we measured it! The second was that when I looked out of the tent, all I could see were rows and rows of trailers where flooded out people were living. I told my team, 'The quicker we do our part and turn in our report, the quicker the levees can be rebuilt and these people can get back into real homes.'"

Tips for Success

Now that you've read some stories, you're ready to write your own. Go ahead. Use the formula. But before you tell your story to anyone, check it over using the suggestions below. The lead-off letters in the tips spell S*U*C*C*E*S*S. The tips will help you make your story the best it can be.

S = *Strategic.* Make sure your story has a purpose and fits your goals. Think about what you want people to know about you or your work, then build your story around that point.

U = *Unique.* Be sure your story helps you stand out from the crowd.

C = *Clear.* Eliminate all the jargon of your profession.

C = *Concrete.* Give a couple of specific details to help your listener see a complete picture. Use specific words; they will stick in the other person's mind more easily than generalities. Don't say "house," say "brick split-level." Don't say, "green," say "chartreuse."

E = *Exciting.* Let your enthusiasm shine through. Use vivid language, an upbeat tone of voice, and a speedy, not "draggy," delivery. Make it memorable.

S = *Short and Succinct.* Use the 5-S formula. You might have a couple of sentences for each of the "Ss." Edit out unnecessary words. Be brief. Never say, "Let's see. Was it Tuesday or Wednesday? No, I think it was Wednesday."

S = *Service-oriented.* Mention the outcome. Who did your actions impact? What was improved, earned, saved, created, streamlined, etc.?

Construct stories on several different topics, then use the one that seems most appropriate to the person you are talking with. As with any skill, you will get better with practice. Challenge yourself to develop one story a week until finding and telling stories has become a conversational habit you feel confident about.

After you tell your story, ask your conversation partner a question that will elicit his or her story. Our favorite question comes from Ann, who asks, "And what are you excited about these days?"

Frequently Asked Questions

Q: *What if I can't think of any stories?*

A: Challenge yourself to notice the moments in your life that you'd like to tell others about. Look for experiences in your leisure and professional life that will show who you are. Listen carefully as others tell stories from their lives. Notice that, for the most part, they are talking about everyday events. Don't think you've got to have earth-shaking stories—like about stopping a runaway train, or winning Best Actor at the Oscars. Just look for times that brought out your best or would illustrate your Character and Competence. Jot down ideas when things happen, so you can hang on to your thoughts until you get a chance to write them out and edit them.

Q: *How can I get into my story? When do I tell it?*

A: Look for a lull in the conversation. Or tell your story in response to "How are you?" or "What's new?" Think of a Segue, a transition sentence that alerts the listener you're about to tell a story.

Q: *What are some tips for shaping my story and making it fun to listen to?*

A: Relive the moment with relish. Craft your story so it paints a vivid picture. The best stories do several things. They reveal your interests, challenges, and talents so that people have an expanded idea of what to call on you for or what to send your way. And they are memorable enough that the listener could repeat them to others with some degree of accuracy. Ask yourself, "Would I want to listen to my story?" Practice it several times, so you get to the point quickly.

Good stories have a turnaround—a moment when you had to do something, come up with a solution, solve a problem. Think of the childhood formula for a good story: "Once upon a time . . . Suddenly . . . Luckily . . . Happily ever after. . . ." If there's not a "happily ever after," can you at least point to a lesson learned?

Q: *Won't people think I'm grandstanding or hotdogging if I tell a story?*

A: No. Good conversationalists know how to pepper their conversation with brief, interesting vignettes about who they are and the experiences they've had. Most people won't be there to see you at your best—how you captured your audience as you spoke at the conference even though the fire alarm went off in the middle of your presentation, or how you survived a camping trip with a dozen eight-year-olds. Think of your story as a gift to the conversation because it offers your conversational partner clues about what topics to bring up next, how to help you, or how to introduce you to others.

"A few years ago," a sports columnist wrote, "I followed Norm Stewart, Mizzou's legendary basketball coach, out of a party. He was stopped by 10 different people. He made every one of those people feel like the most special person in the world. His secret? Always have a good story to tell."

Q: *What if I accidentally tell my story to the same person twice? Or what if someone overhears me telling the same story? That will be embarrassing!*

A: Build a repertoire of stories. Find and tell a new one every week until you have stockpiled enough that you can choose to tell the one that fits the situation or your conversation partner.

Q: *What if everything I do is classified or I work in a profession where confidentiality is very important?*

A: If your work is classified, talk about your role in a generic enough way to meet your organization's guidelines. To respect client confidentiality, disguise the particulars or combine several clients' experiences into one.

Telling a story, whether it's a brief example in your Best/Test or a fully developed 5-S narrative, is an essential networking competency in the Network-Oriented Workplace. Storytelling turns a spotlight on your—or your organization's—success. And it's a skill that you can use and enjoy not only at work, but also in your personal life. One executive taught his teenagers the 5-S formula and found that, finally, he got interesting stories when he asked, "So what's new at school?"

• •

Storytelling turns a spotlight on success.

• •

8

....

Create New Value

Strategic Connections:
Respond to Marketplace Changes

It used to be that, on a typical workday, as many as four highly specialized salespeople would arrive at a single hospital, each one calling on different customers. The salespeople all worked for a company that manufactured a variety of very specialized medical devices. Each salesperson was highly trained—but only in one product line. And each salesperson dealt only with the specialists, surgeons, or patient care professionals who used those particular products.

Then hospitals began changing their way of doing business. They announced they were moving to centralized purchasing systems. This change demanded corresponding changes for the medical device company. No longer could the salesperson deal only with her well-developed contacts for the buying decision.

She had to quickly build additional relationships with people in the purchasing group to complete the sale. And she could no longer act as if she were an "independent." She had to figure out how to relate to and coordinate with others from her company. She had to acknowledge that, "These are our customers, not just my customers." She had to collaborate with other salespeople, be able to cross-sell, and adopt a wider view of what success looked like for her whole organization.

CHANGE ISN'T NEWS. But the speed and scope of change demands more from everyone. There are "changes in target markets, products, business objectives, time frames, cycle times, organizational structure, work location, work teams, job roles, and manager alignment," says "The Rise of the Network Leader," a 2013 Corporate Executive Board publication.

When constant change is the name of the game, relationship building is both more difficult and more necessary. But don't worry. Your networker identity and the full complement of leading-edge skills you have learned position you for success even in this chaotic environment. Competency 8 shows you how to put networking to work to create new value. You already know that networking enables you to do your own job better and faster and to contribute to the achievement of big organizational goals, thus positioning yourself for career advancement.

"Only 30 percent of employees know how they can achieve a broader impact within the organization," says the Corporate Executive Board's 2013 report, "The Rise of The Network Leader." As a strategic networker, you can dramatically improve that sorry statistic as you give and receive the kind of help that's at the heart of collaboration. You can reap the benefits of diversity in your networks, gather—and share—ideas and contacts, and apply your face-to-face networking techniques to build more trusting online relationships. This chapter shows you how to use the face-to-face networking skills you've learned to create real value.

Clarifying Collaboration

Take a look at The Big Picture again (Figure 8–1). Notice that collaboration is the outcome of connecting and conversing. It can only happen when you know how to teach trust, cultivate relationships, and build networks. The 8 Competencies give you the skills you need to do so.

Collaboration was the overwhelming frontrunner on CEOs' wish lists in the 2012 IBM Global Study. When they say they want more collaboration, what are they really asking of you?

Collaboration and teamwork are not the same. To get a clear picture of teamwork, think of a baseball team. The manager (leader) brought you on the team to play a specific position. You're a first baseman, not a pitcher. You're expected to use your first baseman skills. You are not expected to pitch. The games are scheduled long in advance. Rules are followed: three outs, nine innings. Everyone's clear about what constitutes winning. You don't have to like or trust the other players; you just have to do your job.

Collaboration is quite different. You choose to participate. There's no predetermined number of you who come together to collaborate. You all are comfortable playing several different roles depending on what's happening at the moment. Each "game" is unique: You spontaneously address a problem or opportunity that has arisen. Leadership, roles, and time frames are fluid. There's no telling how long the process will take. What constitutes "winning" is not clearly defined. How to get there is even less clear. Collaborators might have competing goals but stay engaged because of an emotional commitment to the undefined outcome. Perhaps most important, trust is at the heart of that emotional commitment. Collaborators trust each other. It's hard to collaborate with Acquaintances and Associates (and almost impossible with Accidents). It's much more likely to happen with Actives,

FIGURE 8-1. The Big Picture

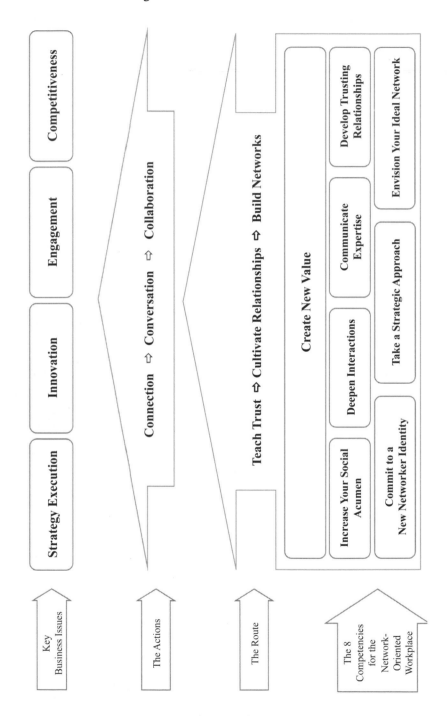

Key Business Issues

Strategy Execution   Innovation   Engagement   Competitiveness

The Actions

Connection ⇪ Conversation ⇪ Collaboration

The Route

Teach Trust ⇪ Cultivate Relationships ⇪ Build Networks

The 8 Competencies for the Network-Oriented Workplace

Create New Value

Increase Your Social Acumen

Deepen Interactions

Communicate Expertise

Develop Trusting Relationships

Commit to a New Networker Identity

Take a Strategic Approach

Envision Your Ideal Network

Advocates, and Allies. A high level of trust is essential because it enables you to take risks and to be vulnerable. Trust provides a safe environment where profitable innovations and good ideas are born.

....

With trust, people take risks and show vul-nerability—both necessary for collaboration.

....

When leaders call for more collaboration, they obviously want more than they have already acquired by buying collaboration soft-ware. We believe they want innovation—the inspired co-creation of new ideas—and outside-the-box thinking, silo smashing and breaking down barriers, less duplication of effort, better use of expertise and resources, and discretionary involvement and engagement.

Your network-based collaborations can provide those outcomes.

Acting on the Three Principles

In this chapter, you'll find out more about putting the three principles to work. Introduced in Chapter 1, here again are the principles that will guide you as you do your job, build your career, and serve your organization.

1. Reframe networking.

2. Risk reaching out.

3. Reinforce the collaborative culture.

REFRAME NETWORKING

The first principle urges you to develop and commit to your new net-worker identity. Add these ideas to your belief system and act on them. Tell yourself:

1. *"I am not my job title."* You're a human being with endless poten-tial and untapped talents. Because you're not just a job title, you're

free to work across boundaries and become known for talents that might not show up in your job description. Marylou is a first-level manager in procurement and someone who is a whiz at learning new software packages. The director of marketing called Marylou and said "Help!" when he was baffled by the new program he was using to prepare a government proposal that had a short turnaround time.

2. *"There is no 'they.'"* You've heard of "they." As in, "When will they . . . ?" "Why don't they . . . ?" Or, "If only they would . . . ." In today's organizations, there's no "they." There's only Bill in IT, or Sue in sales, or Todd in the mailroom.

"They" language takes you off the playing field and relegates you to the sidelines. When you bench yourself, you give up your power or influence. When you make an appointment with Todd in the mailroom to work out a process for receiving those FedEx envelopes the minute they arrive, you're in the game.

3. *"Ideas belong to everyone and to no one."* In a February 2014 *Fast Company* article, author Leo Babauta describes the process of idea generation at Pixar Animation Studios. Your organization can operate like this, too. "When Pixar artists create characters, it's not a matter of one artist sketching out how he thinks a character should look. They all sit around a table, each drawing ideas, putting them in the middle, and others taking those ideas and riffing off them. Dozens and dozens of sketches come out from this process, until they find the one that works best. This means everyone's creativity builds on the creativity of everyone else. This can help you even if you don't have a bunch of other geniuses to work with—find others who are creating cool things, and riff off them, and share your riffs." So whether you're trying to streamline the hiring process or invent new ways to work with vendors, adopt the belief that ideas are abundant and spring up faster when you collaborate with others.

4. *"I seek out people unlike myself."* Lynnette got a LinkedIn invitation from a woman who said, "We know 56 of the same people. Let's

Link!" *Hmmmmm.* . . . Attractive offer? Maybe. It's comfortable to hang out with people who are like you and who know the people you know. But Lynnette wondered if she wouldn't rather expand her circles, if she wouldn't be more likely to find business value if she spent time and energy getting to know people outside of her usual crowd.

Your WorkNet, OrgNet, ProNet, and LifeNet should assure you of a well-balanced array of contacts. If many of the people in your Nets have backgrounds and experiences similar to yours, be sure to add diversity to your definition of networking (and reread Chapter 3). Think about the possibilities. You can intentionally diversify your contacts with regard to age, race, gender, geography, function, culture, and interests.

> *Diversify contacts with regard to age, race, gender, geography, function, culture, and interest.*

Diversity is its own reward. But Ron Burt says it also brings new value. Burt is a professor at the University of Chicago's Booth School of Business where he researches the benefits of networking. Here are a few of the advantages Burt's research promises you'll enjoy when your network is made up of people with a wide variety of backgrounds, from a wide variety of arenas. You'll:

- Move information faster and to more people.

- Spend less time and energy to get good results.

- Create tailored solutions instead of relying on one-size-fits-all answers.

- Hear about opportunities that expand your horizons and your skill sets.

- Be paid better and promoted faster.

Easier said than done? Use the strategies that follow to add more diversity your networks:

• *Provoke serendipity.* At least once a day, reach out and start a conversation with someone you haven't met. Jason, who usually sat on the third row with the same group of buddies during the CEO's monthly briefings, decided to sit in the last row, thinking, "I wonder who sits way back here?" Sure, it seemed like a small change, but he met a new person from a department he didn't know much about.

• *Go to somebody else's conference.* Sylvia had gone to the same annual conference for engineers for the past 11 years. Since she worked with lots of architects, this year she decided to attend the annual meeting of the American Institute of Architects. The new perspectives she found paid off as she interacted with architects in her firm and had a better understanding of their priorities and approaches. And one of her conference connections with expertise in designing churches partnered with her firm to bid on a megachurch project.

• *Focus on special interests.* Aasif, who works in finance, has a son with Down syndrome. He wondered how to encourage his firm to support the Special Olympics. He did some background research about the charity work of other companies. He talked with people in his OrgNet who were involved in deciding how corporate contributions funds would be spent. He built a network with several other parents in the company who had mentally and physically challenged kids. Together they launched an initiative that resulted in company sponsorship of the New Jersey State Special Olympics. A side benefit was that Aasif and the others in the Special Olympics network met new people throughout their company who became potential collaborators on other projects.

• *Cultivate your curiosity.* Look in the newspaper or online for information about a meeting of a group you've never been involved with. After seeing the troubles his brother had gone through, Wayne was committed to helping veterans get back into the civilian job market. He went to a gathering of volunteers of Hire Heroes USA and was introduced to a whole new circle of contacts. When Wayne liked what he saw, he encouraged people in personnel in his company to partner with Hire Heroes and soon a hiring initiative was launched.

 * *Tap your talents.* Pursue a passion or hobby that will put you in touch with a whole new set of people. Andrea had always sung in church choirs, but when she heard about a jazz singing class for aspiring divas, she signed up. Andrea connected with a whole new circle of people who were very unlike her—though they had a love of jazz in common.

Diversifying Our Contacts

"As VP of Human Resources I think it's very important that we connect and build relationships across the whole company. I wondered how extensive and diverse my 10-member team's contacts actually were. I asked them to list the 10 people they knew best in the organization—people outside of HR, training, and talent management. I said, 'Tell me who you go to when you want to get something done, find out what's happening, vet an idea, or influence business processes and initiatives.'

"When everyone compared their lists, we noticed that of the 100 names, only 58 were unique. The other 42 were repeats. Frankly, we were all surprised at our limited 'reach.' I asked them, 'What do you think this means for our visibility and ability to stay in touch with wider business issues and trends? If we all know the same 58 people, doesn't that affect our capacity to partner with and influence our business unit customers?'

"They decided that they needed to expand and diversify their networks, to include people of different ages, levels, functions, and locations. They came up with three strategies:

1. Ask good contacts in their OrgNets, 'Who should I be talking with in marketing, or IT, or wherever?'

2. Find ways to serve on a task force or work in other parts of the organization to meet new people.

3. Reach out at every opportunity—in the cafeteria, in a training class, or at a cross-functional meeting—to start conversations and teach people what to come to our team for.

RISK REACHING OUT

Creative entrepreneur Nick Onken built his photography career working for giants like Nike, Coca Cola, and Lamborghini. He says, "You're only growing when you're playing out of your comfort zone. To close the gap between where you are and what you envision requires discomfort." Your new networking skills will give you the confidence to raise the stakes and step out of your comfort zone. Here are four ways to create new value and act on the second principle, risk reaching out.

#1. Be a great connector. Wharton Professor Adam Grant says, "Despite the power of introductions, people often overlook introductions as a form of giving." He was quoted in an August 2013 Huffington Post article, "The Giving Habits of Americans." The article gives the results of a poll showing that rather than making introductions, "people are more likely to give help, knowledge, recognition, money, mentoring, and skills. Only 27 percent of Americans had made an introduction in the past year." Decide that it's your job to connect people, both inside and outside your organization and across your Four Nets.

#2. Make the investment pay off. Strategic connectors know that networking is not an event; it's a way of being with people. But much valuable networking does take place at events like conferences, professional

meetings, and social activities. Because you want to spend your time and money wisely, ask yourself, "What's the dollar amount I'll spend (or my organization will spend for me) this year to provide me with venues for extending my networks? How can I make sure I'm getting a return on that investment?"

What was the return on investment (ROI) for your networking expenditures last year? First you have to figure out much you "invested." What were the places you went to find clients, learn more about best practices, hear about current business information that could affect the bottom line, or make your company more visible? To project your expenditures for this year, add up the amounts you spent last year on clubs, events, dues, memberships, trade shows, conferences, professional meetings, company retreats, receptions, luncheons, golf outings—any activity where your purpose was to build relationships for increased sales, to stay current in your field, or to find and share resources.

Devise a system to document that you are getting your money's worth. Make sure you are keeping careful track of the benefits that have accrued—to you, to your team, to your project, to the bottom line.

Look for ways to increase your ROI. Figure out how to make sure the outcomes do more than merely offset what you spend.

#3. Find the BringBack. Much of networking focuses on outreach, but there's a flip side. In today's organizations, you are responsible for gathering valuable information and resources on the outside and distributing what you found on the inside. That's your BringBack. Finding the BringBack means:

- Keeping your antennae up and being on the alert for anything that would be useful.

- Taking the initiative to determine who needs to receive it.

- Giving it in a way that encourages the recipient to use it.

You'll find BringBack at all kinds of networking events, through reading, and online. You may come across it serendipitously, or you may go looking for it when you see a need. Or as you teach people in any of your Nets what you are looking for and interested in, they may present you with it.

* *

Networking involves not only outreach, but BringBack.

* *

Figuring out who needs the information you've found may be easy. You may know that Will is interested in online recruiting. You hear about a resource or an article and give it to him. Or you may discover something you're sure is valuable, but not know who needs it. Ask some of your contacts. You're sure to come up with the right person.

How to give your BringBack may be tricky. People worry that they might be stepping on someone's toes or offering something that people already know about. Those kinds of worries inhibit the flow of information. Risk reaching out. Say, "I ran across something I thought you might find useful. May I send it to you?" Make sure what you offer contains enough specific information (correctly spelled name, telephone number, email address, website, etc.) that the recipient can follow up and check it out.

Look at the impact Janna and Yelena were able to have as a result of keeping their eyes and ears open for information and introductions that might help others.

At a Chamber of Commerce meeting, Janna, a CPA, learned that the new membership director wanted to reach out to young people in the business community and was interested in starting a group for them. Janna took that information back to a meeting of her practice area. The firm decided to buy a corporate membership in the Chamber and invest time and energy in support of HYPE (Helping

Young Professionals Engage). The involvement by Janna and a few others from the firm brought many rewards: visibility in the community, new business leads, professional development opportunities, and eventually an award from the Chamber for their support.

Yelena, a software manager from one of the major international underwriters, spoke at a convention on new developments in cyber insurance. After hearing Yelena's presentation, Julie introduced herself. Over lunch, Julie said that the credit union where she was a manager was worried about security breaches and needed the upgrades Yelena had described. Julie and Yelena got on their smartphones. They made email introductions to the right people in each of their companies, so the conversation could continue.

We don't want to leave the topic of BringBack without giving some tips about how to boost your BringBack from conferences. In fact, we suggest you make a copy of these tips and hang it near your desk. Read it again the next time you're going to a conference.

A conference puts you face to face. Take advantage of proximity to create the interactions that make the time and money you spend worthwhile.

- *Figure out what you want to Get.* Before you even leave town, jot down what you want to find: answers to challenges, solutions to problems, resources you need, and people you'd like to meet.

- *Take along other people's Agendas.* Get more bang for your buck and build your relationships with colleagues who aren't going to the conference. Collect their concerns, add them to your Get list, and hunt for answers for them.

- *Get ready to Give.* Fill out the other side of your Agenda—what you want to share with the people you meet: new resources, your special expertise, solutions to problems, and recent innovations and projects your organization is involved in.

- *Design your own session.* Before the conference, contact a speaker, a leader, an expert, or a counterpart from a similar organization and plan to get together. At the conference, ask interesting people you meet if they'd like to get together for dinner. Tell them to meet you at 6 P.M. in the lobby. Then go out to dinner with a dozen new contacts.

- *Agree to split up.* If other people you know from your company or professional association are going, decide in advance *not* to attend the same sessions and hang out with each other. Plan beforehand how you'll deploy yourselves, cover as many sessions as you can, and share notes afterward.

- *Put ideas to use.* Get together with colleagues, either at the conference or afterward and have a "how are we going to apply this" brainstorming session.

- *Pick sessions carefully.* Focus on the knowledge you need and the skills you want to develop. Look for the right sessions that will force you to reevaluate, plan for the future, and expand your horizons.

- *Ask the speaker.* Let the experts help you solve a problem or meet a challenge. Ask the speaker out for coffee or link up with a couple of other attendees and set up a breakfast or lunch.

- *Volunteer for a job at the conference.* Helping out makes it easy to meet people, gain professional visibility, mingle with the leaders, and build a worldwide network. Choose your job carefully so that it helps you, not hides you in the back room. When Tim volunteered to pick up the general session keynoter at the airport, he had no idea that he'd be chauffeuring—and chatting with—Indra Nooyi, the CEO of PepsiCo.

- *Find the big idea.* Look for the one great idea that you can bring back and think of a way to present it to key people in the most effective way.

#4. *Expand your OrgNet.* "Some 86 percent of senior leaders say that working across boundaries inside and outside their companies is extremely important. Just 7 percent, however, believe they are very effective at it," says a 2011 Center for Creative Leadership paper, "Declaration of Interdependence."

We've also noticed that people's OrgNets are often underdeveloped. There are a couple of reasons people may avoid this kind of boundary spanning. In the past, your organization may have had impenetrable walls between departments. Those walls formed "silos" or "stovepipes" that were hard to break out of. Now, with the command-and-control mode fading away, those walls are tumbling down. You may, however, still feel a reluctance to engage with people beyond your own area. Also, OrgNet contacts may be people who have job titles that are higher than yours on the organization chart. Talking "up" may feel uncomfortable (see Chapter 6, "Talking Up the Ladder," for ideas). But your networker identity and new skills will make it easier when you decide it's time to strengthen your OrgNet.

How Strong Is Your OrgNet?

Use these questions to think about the strength of your current OrgNet:

1. Do you know people at all levels of the organization? Do they know your name and what you do?

2. Do you know all the people whose work intersects yours in any way?

3. Do you know people who have jobs you might like to have someday?

4. Are you involved in any cross-functional efforts or interdepartmental activities (temporary assignments, committees, task forces, special projects, and volunteer activities)?

5. Are you plugged into the grapevine? Do you find out what's up before it's officially announced?

6. Do you take every opportunity to meet face to face to define and discuss complex problems, shifting priorities, areas of responsibility?

7. Do you know and talk with others about tools to get the job done today and trends that will impact your job and your organization in the future?

8. Do you have effective internal channels through which to send information?

9. When you see a problem that involves people from various areas, do you take the initiative to bring them together to solve it?

10. Do you drop by to see people—even when you don't need anything?

REINFORCE THE COLLABORATIVE CULTURE

"Be the change you want to see." That's more than an inspiring bumper sticker. It's good advice from revered Indian political and spiritual leader, Mahatma Gandhi. And it's the third principle in a nutshell. Act as if you own the organization. You make it what it is. Behaving as if the Network-Oriented Workplace is a reality is the way to make it real—and successful. If there's a problem in your organization, don't wait for others to take the lead. The business world is so competitive that you can't afford to wait around hoping someone else will unsnarl a process that doesn't work or uncover an emerging customer concern. You're always in charge of taking the next step. Your innovation, your idea, the network you pull together could mean that your company wins a huge contract.

To make a difference, ask yourself the questions that follow:

How can I cut expenses? Les and Siddhartha were talking one day and wondered what the company was spending on individual bottles of water. They also worried about the negative footprint the plastic was making on the environment. The two colleagues asked their company to order and strategically place several water coolers and posted signs encouraging people to use their own coffee mugs and water bottles. Les and Siddhartha were acting like they owned the company or at least were in charge of the "supplies" budget. And in acting like that, they were.

How can I conserve resources? It's easy to get used to the free flow of resources and supplies, but in the Network-Oriented Workplace, it's your responsibility to keep an eye on the bottom line. In an October 2013 *Forbes Magazine* article, Meghan Casserly interviews CEOs about lessons learned. Founder and chairman Jim Koch, CEO of Boston Beer Company, told how he came up with *his* "string theory." "In the middle of graduate school, I decided to take a break and became an instructor with Outward Bound. At the beginning of each four-week course I gave everyone a supply of Alpine cord (a kind of string for lashing gear, pitching tarps, etc.). Consistently, if I gave my group plenty of string, they would run out and need more. But, if I gave them less and told them they had only two-thirds of what they really needed, they would get incredibly creative and make that cord last. They'd splice, they'd share, they'd save; they'd forage for bits of rope left behind by others. Since we were on a tight budget in the early days, we used every piece of 'string' we had, and that created a corporate culture of innovation and creativity."

How can I eliminate redundancies? As you get out of your silo and expand your OrgNet you're bound to come across duplications of efforts and initiatives. When Susan got involved in leadership of the Women's Network she realized that her company could save time and money by combining the orders for supplies for all nine Employee Affinity Groups. Everybody needed things like signs, nametags, and conference notebooks with imprinted logos. She also suggested to leaders of the other groups that they use the same caterer for all their events and save money with a volume discount.

How can I invent a new or improved process? Jo was asked to design a web-based orientation course for new hires. While she knew this change was motivated by budget cuts, she had a problem with the idea. She knew the "content" could be delivered in a podcast, but the bonding and relationship building that used to go on in her face-to-face classes would be missing, making the experience much less powerful. So she decided to create a cadre of Guides within the company. To this handpicked group she said, "When you become a new hire's Guide, I want you to make sure he or she meets at least seven key contacts within the first month—two peers, two people in other divisions, two people who are two levels above them, and one 'wild card'—anyone you choose." By "meet" Jo explained that she meant a face-to-face (or if absolutely necessary, online) lunch meeting that would help the new person feel connected and acclimated.

How can I share what I have? When Ted couldn't keep his temporary assistant busy for the whole day, he sent an email to others on his floor saying, "José has a couple of hours this afternoon. If you have a task he can do for you at his desk, please let me know." Rachel, who works for a start-up handbag company in New York City, showed her sensitivity to scarce resources and the need for quick turnaround times when she told coworkers, "Late Monday I'm flying to San Francisco for two days. If you have any bags that need to get to the West Coast office quickly, I have extra space in my suitcase and can get them there by Tuesday morning."

Build Trust Online

In today's technology-driven world of work, you will often have the opportunity to create important value without ever meeting your colleagues and partners in person. When you say "yes" to a linking or friending request, you have an online connection. Or you may have virtual coworkers or teammates you didn't choose, but who are part of your WorkNet. Turning these connections into trusting relationships takes more than a click. You can move from the Associate Stage to the Active, Advocate, or even Ally Stages with your online connections when you apply the same trust-building strategies you use to develop face-to-face relationships. Even when—or especially when—you are connecting online, teaching your contact about your Character and Competence is essential. When trust is established, you have a base for true collaboration.

> *Apply your face-to-face trust-building strategies online, too.*

Gartner, the world's leading information technology research and advisory company, predicts that through 2015, "80 percent of social business efforts will not achieve the intended benefits due to inadequate leadership and overemphasis on technology." In a January 2013 press release, Carol Rozwell, Vice President of Gartner said, "There is too much focus on content and technology, and not enough focus on leadership and relationships." Users are understandably wary of technologies that tout instant access to anyone, anywhere, anytime, with no regard for the Stage of Trust that they have reached with their contacts.

Whether you're using internal social networking tools or external systems like LinkedIn, Facebook, Instagram, Pinterest, and Twitter, follow these guidelines to show the kind of Character and Competence that says, "Even though you and I haven't met (or rarely meet) face to face, you can trust me." Here are some guidelines for trust-building online:

• *Show up human.* Add words and phrases that show a wide variety of feelings. Have you ever said to an online contact, "I'm curious about. . . ." Or, "I was so surprised to see that . . . ." Or, "I'm excited at the prospect of. . . ." Since facial expression and body language are missing in digital communications, your at-a-distance contacts need those clues about what your face might be saying if they could only see it.

• *Earn the right.* When you ask for help, be sure you've earned the right to ask for that level of commitment, or time, or trust. Kena chose 22 photos for a marketing brochure. She selected five people in her OrgNet—all people with extensive customer contact—to take a look online and give her feedback on the photos. Kena made sure, since the process would take time, to involve people she'd helped in the past. Their responses led her to reject three of the photos and choose new ones that didn't provoke unwanted associations in the viewers' minds.

• *Keep agreements.* When you promise something, deliver. Timely, well-thought-out, and accurate responses show a lot about who you are and why you can be trusted. Just because you're using a machine interface doesn't mean your promises are any less important.

• *Share your contacts.* But be sure you've done your homework. Maretta saw that Anthony had requested ideas on how to find good speakers for the CEO's retreat for top salespeople. She wanted to recommend a speaker she'd heard, but first checked out the speaker's website, looked at his LinkedIn profile, and talked with a couple of others who'd heard his presentation. When she'd confirmed all her hunches, she got back online to give Anthony the speaker's name and contact information, along with a strong endorsement.

• *Give appropriately.* Until you've gotten to know an online contact, be careful about the private information you reveal. And limit your offers of help until you develop the relationship. People may question your Character and Competence if you overenthusiastically or prematurely overwhelm them with your generosity.

• *Tell stories.* In Chapter 7, you learned the 5-S formula for constructing a story. That formula will help you come up with stories that teach something important about what you've done and who you are. Keep your stories short and upbeat. In online communications, there's often a sense of urgency and a feeling of "we don't have time for that." Stories help you teach about your Character and Competence and learn the same about your contacts.

• *Find the humor.* Putting a smiley face emoticon into your message is one way to do it, but try coming up with something that shows a more personal touch. What would make the recipient smile? When the project Jon and Ray were leading was giving them headaches, Jon, recalling what comedian Groucho Marx once said, sent this message to Ray: "Only some of us can learn from other people's mistakes. The rest of us have to *be* the other people." On the other hand, be cautious about sending professional contacts those dog or cat videos you think are so adorable.

• *Show you're listening.* Just as in face-to-face conversations, it's a sign of respect when you do or say something to signal that you've been paying attention to what contacts have told you about their lives at work or outside. Alida said, "How's your MBA program going?" Gene asked, "How are plans for your trip to Lisbon next month coming along?"

• *Be tactful.* Some people think that just because they're not face to face, they have a license to be brutally honest. Just as in your face-to-face relationships, handling conflict with kindness and generosity shows your Character. Isaac Newton, mathematician and scientist, got it right 300 years ago when he said, "Tact is the knack of making a point without making an enemy."

• *Suggest a face-to-face meeting.* If time, distance, and budgets don't allow an actual onsite, use FaceTime or Skype or one of the other tools for "seeing" each other. A visual meeting like that will warm up a relationship and make it easier to collaborate with renewed energy. Be clear about the purpose of the meeting, so you don't waste time, but also take time to get to know each other. People at one of the Big Four accounting firms are encouraged to chat a bit before getting down to work. They ask questions such as, "How's your weekend shaping up? Got any plans?" Or, "How did you all fare in the big snowstorm last week?"

Mentor and Model

Have you ever stopped to notice the connection between the words "courage" and "encourage"? A little encouragement from others gives you the courage to be a better networker and collaborator. Cultivate a "one-for-all, all-for-one" mindset. Recognize that the more you and your colleagues look out for each other, the healthier your organization will be.

Use these strategies to mentor others and model the behavior you want to see:

Give special attention to those you know the best. It's easy to take for granted the people you work with all the time. You do your job. Your coworkers do theirs. Routines set in. Everyone's super busy. It's hard to find time to relax, explore, and kick ideas around—the very behaviors that result in innovation. So find time to slow down, to look out and look up from all the details. Josh, the department director, announced that every Friday he was open for a YOLO Lunch. "What's that?" everybody wondered. Josh said, "Bring your lunch, come to the conference room, and find out." YOLO ("you only live once") turned out to be a free-for-all for exploring new ideas. "The only ground rule is," Josh said, "don't talk about current projects." Taking his lead, people came up with topics like these: "If we were to reconfigure our workspace, what would it look like and what could it accomplish?" and "What's the least productive time of day for you and what could reenergize you?" The discussions resulted in surfacing problems and making changes for the better.

Convene a "coaching club." Invite a few people you like from your WorkNet and OrgNet to a Best/Test brainstorm. Give everybody a turn to answer the "What do you do?" question and then give suggestions on how to make those answers even more memorable, interesting, and reflective of their Character and Competence. Often it's hard for people to get enough distance from what they do to come up with a good answer. And coaching others will help you see how to make your answers better. And Mattias and George found that they could borrow each other's answers when telling prospects about their firm's accomplishments.

Offer "ride-alongs." Debbie had just been made a vice president at the consulting firm she worked for. She remembered how hard it was to imagine going on sales calls when she first started with the firm 16 years ago. So she made it a point to invite one of the junior staffers to come along with her when she visited a prospect. As they traveled back to the office, she talked with the person about his impressions. She also told about how she transitioned from thinking of herself solely as an expert in mergers to seeing herself as someone who could bring in the business.

Encourage what you like. When you see someone do something that helps people or helps your organization, appreciate it. In animal trainer Karen Pryor's book *Don't Shoot the Dog,* she shows that, rather than punishing or ignoring behavior you don't like, the best thing to do is encourage what you *do* like. Mike said to Reza, "I couldn't have made that deadline without you. Thanks! And what I really appreciated is that you stayed so cheerful and upbeat—even when it got to be 11 P.M.!"

Value asking as much as giving. How many times have you heard someone say, "I got as much out of being a mentor as I did from being mentored?" Learn to ask for help as well as giving it. Who better to help you figure out a good next step for reaching out to a prospect than others who know you well? Who better to help you strategize who to add to your OrgNet than your coworker?

Team up at events. Jake, an expert on business valuation, and Tomas, an expert on taxes for nonprofits, worked for the same CPA firm. They made three agreements before going to a two-day conference. First, they agreed to split up and try to meet lots of new people. Second, Jake said, "Since I know the kinds of people you'd like to meet and you know the same about me, let's be on the lookout for people that we can introduce to each other." And finally, they agreed to give each other feedback after the conference. Tomas said, "Here's a better client example to use when you introduce me to others." Jake said, "Tomas, I know you think the fact that you look so young means people won't take you seriously, but when you meet someone, I think you'll put them at ease more quickly and warm things up if you include a smile with your handshake."

Never go off duty. That sounds daunting, doesn't it, but it's true. There are no time-outs, no breaks, no excuses when it comes to modeling behavior you want to encourage in others. As philosopher Albert Schweitzer once said, "Example is not the main thing in influencing others—it's the only thing." On a Wednesday afternoon at IDEO, a design and consulting firm, someone from the C-suite joined a team for a brainstorming session. "His arrival in the room signaled strongly that helping is an expected behavior in the culture and that everyone is part of the helping network," reported a January/February 2014 *Harvard Business Review* article about how the firm reinforces its helping culture.

Seek out heroes. Find people to learn from and put yourself in situations where others can just naturally mentor you. Michael Dell, CEO and founder of Dell, Inc., one of the world's leading sellers of personal computers, advises, "If you're the smartest person in the room, find a different room."

As you put the three principles to work, you create additional organizational benefits from your networking and reap career advantages for yourself.

9

·····················

How to Develop and Support Your Network-Oriented Workplace

THIS CHAPTER is written for leaders who want to move from the old command-and-control way of working toward a more collaborative culture. But no matter what your role or level, you'll benefit from getting a look at what leaders are thinking and how you can contribute more to your organization's success.

Strategic Connections focuses on how to create the face-to-face relationships, built on trust, that lead to the most productive collaboration. We asked a leader at a large consulting firm, "How do you make sure your employees know how to develop trust with each other?" Looking surprised, he replied, "It's part of our corporate mandate!"

After reading this book, you won't assume that just because you tell people to collaborate they'll know how to do it and will leap into action. Listing "a collaborative culture" as a company imperative or value isn't enough. Why? Because trust-building, the precondition for collaboration, is a *learned* skill set, one that involves specific steps and nuanced concepts.

In any relationship, the risk you're willing to take and the value you derive are both determined by the Stage of Trust you've reached. The challenge arises because most people don't have any system or method for gauging the Stage of Trust they've achieved or for managing the trust-building process.

The 8 Competencies featured in the first eight chapters of this book deliver the trust-building methodologies and best networking practices you need. As employees master these state-of-the-art skills, your calls for increased collaboration will no longer fall on deaf ears.

In this chapter, you'll learn how to assess the networker identity of your organization. It's a product of your systems, policies, and workplace climate. You'll discover ways to develop and support your employees as they connect, converse, and collaborate to create the new value on which your organization depends for future success.

Are you seeing the demise of command-and-control and the rise of the connected, collaborative workplace? It's the next big advance in the evolution of organizations. Many people and organizations are heralding the coming of the Network-Oriented Workplace. In this book, we quote thinkers who are exploring it—Alex Pentland, Ben Waber, Rob Cross, Ron Burt, Adam Grant—and organizations that are sketching its broad outlines—The Conference Board, the Corporate Executive Board, McKinsey, IBM, and many others.

A Network-Oriented Workplace doesn't happen automatically. You can't buy it. You can't mandate it. But when you tear down the barriers and build up the foundation and infrastructure, you can create the environment in which employees can build, enhance and strengthen their networks—individual networks from which your organization will realize substantial benefits.

And the Word Is . . .

Because of its historical connections with job-hunting, careering, and sales, the term "networking" may put people off. We've noticed, as we've talked with leaders in corporations, professional services firms, and government agencies, that some are substituting other terms for "networking," like "partnering," "horizontal integration," "silo-smashing," "relationship management," "social acumen," "connectivity," "teamwork," and even "collaboration."

We see collaboration as the *outcome* of networking, not synonymous with it. Our definition has evolved over the two decades we've been teaching networking skills:

> Networking is the deliberate and discretionary process of creating, cultivating, and capitalizing on trust-based, mutually beneficial relationships for individual and organizational success.

The Need for a Network-Oriented Workplace

"I am convinced we have the right strategy. I am convinced we have the right offerings. I am convinced we have the right people. But what keeps me awake at night is the ability of people in my organization to work together to deliver." That's what the CEO of a multinational telecommunications company in South Asia said.

As we talk with other C-suite leaders in companies across the globe, we hear the same frustrations about how their organizations fail to optimize their potential because their people fail to work together effectively. What's happening in your organization? Are you satisfied with your people's strategy execution, innovation, engagement, and competiveness?

THE FAILURE OF STRATEGY EXECUTION

In 2013, the Economist Intelligence Unit issued a report, "Why Good Strategies Fail: Lessons for the C-Suite." The research queried 587 senior executives around the globe and found that 61 percent acknowledged that their firms struggle to bridge the gap between strategy formulation and its day-to-day implementation.

A May 2000 *Harvard Business Review* article, "Cracking the Code of Change," puts the failure rate even higher. Authors Michael Beer and Nitin Nohria write, "Despite some individual successes . . . change remains difficult to pull off, and few companies manage the process as well as they would like. Most of their initiatives—installing new technology, downsizing, restructuring, or trying to change corporate culture—have had low success rates. The brutal fact is that about 70 percent of all change initiatives fail."

What's the reason for these abysmal statistics? In their 2010 book, *Strategic Speed: Mobilize People, Accelerate Execution*, authors Jocelyn Davis, Henry Frechette, and Edwin Boswell researched organizations around the world that were considered successful at speedy strategy execution. The researchers discovered that the "X-factor" that determined success was the attention their leaders paid, not to strategy development, process improvement, or installing new technologies, but to people.

The X-factor is the attention leaders pay to people.

THE STAGNATION OF INNOVATION

In a *Business Week* article, "CEOs Say Investing in Innovation Is Not Paying Off," author Bernhard Warner says only 18 percent of CEOs are happy with their results; the other 82 percent are disappointed. What goes wrong?

You may have heard the empty box story. This classic tale also points to the people factor. Consumers complained about buying boxes of soap and finding them empty. To solve the problem, engineers were told to find a way to spot the empties among the boxes flowing along on the assembly line on their way to the shipping department. The assembly line workers watched the engineers working away. Nobody asked the workers for a solution. Over many months, the engineers developed an x-ray machine with high-resolution monitors crewed by two people to identify the empty boxes. The cost? Astronomical!

One day, as they waited for the new equipment to be installed, a worker found an industrial fan sitting unused in a storage closet. He brought it to the assembly line and switched it on. When the blast of air hit a box that was empty, it flew off the line. Problem solved.

"Innovation only occurs in a 'sympathetic environment,'" say authors Jeff Mauzy and Richard Harriman in their book, *Creativity, Inc.: Building an Inventive Organization.* "The ideal creative climate nurtures intrinsic motivation, assures the safety necessary for curiosity, holds high expectations for creativity, and provides the support critical to evaluation."

THE PROBLEM OF ENGAGEMENT

You're probably painfully aware of the statistics. Gallup Inc.'s worldwide studies in 2013 covered 1.4 million workers in 34 countries. Only 13 percent of employees were "engaged"—psychologically committed to their jobs and organizations and likely to be making positive contributions. Some 63 percent were "not engaged"—lacking the motivation to invest their energies to achieve their organizations' goals. And the second largest group of 25 percent were classified as "actively disengaged"—unhappy, unproductive, and likely to spread negativity.

Jack Welch, former CEO of General Electric, said, "There are only three measurements that tell you nearly everything you need to know about your organization's overall performance: employee engagement, customer satisfaction, and cash flow. . . . It goes without saying that no company, small or large, can win over the long run without energized employees who believe in the mission and understand how to achieve it."

One of our associates told us about an exercise he devised for a leadership workshop. He divided the participants in half. In a whisper, he told one group, "You are Renters" and the other, "You are Homeowners." Both groups were given the same situations to respond to:

- A water stain has appeared on the kitchen ceiling.

- The paint on the exterior of the house is beginning to peel.

- Robberies in the area are on the increase and your next-door neighbor is the most recent victim.

The responses from the two groups were diametrically opposed. The Renters said they'd make a formal complaint to the landlord, withhold the rent until the problem was fixed, and leave the neighborhood. The Homeowners, on the other hand, said they'd fix the stain themselves, ask friends over to help paint the house one weekend, and talk to the neighbors about setting up a neighborhood watch group.

Sadly, the reality is that most people in organizations are "Renters." They lack a feeling of ownership in the business. They are *un*engaged.

THE CHALLENGE OF COMPETITION

Competitiveness includes making the most of your resources. In a workshop in Sydney, we asked a group of leaders, "What does the lack of networking cost you?" An executive from a large bank jumped in and said, "I can answer that question for you with a specific number. We've just completed an internal audit to determine the costs of duplication of processes, based on various parts of the bank doing their own thing and not leveraging what someone else already has done. The cost of that duplication? $35 million!" What does the lack of networking competency cost your company?

Competitiveness also includes making the most of your human capital. Many organizations are asking a wide range of employees, not just the sales force, to bring in the business. The COO of an IT company in India said, "The people who are most intimate with the customer's business are our project managers working on customers' sites. They are absolutely in the best position to identify potential incremental business opportunities. Although we have asked and keep asking them to keep their eyes and ears open for business opportunities, nothing is happening. I have come to the realization that we need a minor revolution for them to really embrace the business development aspects of their job. Merely directing them to do this is not enough."

Unfortunately, that COO's experience is not unusual. People in what we've labeled "the quiet careers," such as engineering, accounting, and IT, are particularly resistant to taking on a business development role. They often see "selling" as incompatible with their professional identity and lack the skills to uncover opportunities.

All of these areas of concern—strategy execution, innovation, engagement, and competitiveness—have something in common. All can be impacted by improving face-to-face networking on the part of employees.

Take another look at The Big Picture in Chapter 8 for an overview of how to achieve greater collaboration. As employees master The 8 Competencies, they learn how to teach trust, cultivate relationships, and build networks. They connect, they converse, and ultimately, they collaborate to contribute to the big business issues.

What's Your Organization's Networker Identity?

In Chapter 1, we explained the process individuals go through as they commit to a networker identity. Organizations also need to go through the process of finding their networker identity. Use the diagram to pinpoint where your organization is now and see the possibilities.

The horizontal axis on Figure 9–1 shows the continuum of attitudes your organization might hold toward networking. That continuum ranges from *Discouraging* through *Encouraging* to *Committed*.

In organizations that are Discouraging, leaders are unaware of the benefits strong employee networks can deliver. Leaders, still in a command-and-control mode, may seriously doubt whether internal and external networking are legitimate business activities. Leaders are uncomfortable with networking because they don't feel they can control it. Policies and procedures act as barriers to networking, and it's both disregarded and unrewarded.

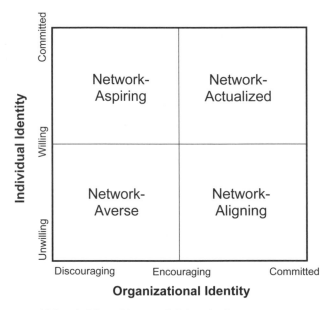

FIGURE 9-1. *What's Your Network Identity?*

In organizations that are Encouraging, leaders have discovered the value of employee networks, are removing barriers and disincentives, and are putting many support systems in place. Typically, these organizations have spent considerable money on technologies for connecting and collaborating. Overshadowed by these technologies, face-to-face networking may not yet be highly valued. Leaders may wrongly believe that employees have all the skills they need to network and collaborate and that simply asking them to put those skills to work will get results.

> **Leaders may wrongly believe that employees have networking skills.**

In organizations that are Committed, leaders expect collaboration; act as role models for networking; remove barriers to connecting up, down, and across the organization; and revise policies and systems so they are "networking-friendly." Once organizations have reached this level of commitment, they have aligned their environment with their intentions.

But intentions, infrastructure, and imperatives alone are not enough. When organizations call for collaboration without developing the skills and the networker identities of employees, their aspirations remain unrealized.

At the center of building a Network-Oriented Workplace is *training*. Leaders who want to reinforce the importance of face-to-face networking as a high-value business strategy recognize that building the capacity and competence of employees is essential. This training gives employees the specific skills and enterprise-wide focus necessary for their—and their organization's—success.

On the vertical axis in Figure 9–1, you can see the continuum of employee attitudes, from *Unwilling* through *Willing* to *Committed*. This continuum reflects the attitudes of employees toward the value of face-to-face networking and reveals their beliefs about whether they personally can use networking to make a difference, not only for themselves, but also to benefit their organizations.

Employees who are Unwilling typically focus on tasks more than on relationships and have negative mindsets—for a host of reasons—toward networking. These employees see themselves as non-networkers. They may feel that networking conflicts with their image of themselves as professionals. Many classify themselves as shy or introverted and don't realize that networking skills are competencies that they can learn.

Employees who are Willing recognize that networking could help them get their jobs done and advance their careers. As organizations demand more in the way of collaboration and business development from them, these employees decide that they need to get on board. They are ready to take on the role of networker, if only they knew how. Though open to the idea of networking, they haven't yet felt comfortable and confident with the network-building process. They need the organizational acknowledgment and support that only you can give.

Employees who are Committed are convinced of the value of building trust-based relationships with people inside and outside their organizations. They know that networking is skill-based, not inborn and not limited by personality type. They are seeking ways to collaborate with others to improve everybody's results. These employees believe that they could contribute more to their organization's success. But the impact they can deliver is unrealized because the organizational environment doesn't yet elicit their best.

Use the diagram to analyze where your organization and your employees are now. Are they:

- *Network-Averse?* You have unwilling, unskilled employees and an environment that discourages people from cultivating and capitalizing on networking.

- *Network-Aligning?* Leaders are committed to the value of networking. Connecting technologies are ubiquitous, and policies and procedures are being revamped to support a networking culture. This is a fertile environment, but your employees are dragging their feet. Leaders may assume that employees lack motivation, but what they really lack is know-how and the opportunity to develop their network identities. Their resistance means that you don't get the outcome you want when you say, "Collaborate."

- *Network-Aspiring?* Your employees are willing to believe in or have committed to the value of networking. They are eager to use networking to get their work done and to advance their careers, but are missing that wide-angle view that helps them see how to work on initiatives and goals beyond their own jobs. Since organizational policies are unfriendly, most networking is "under the radar." It's still an untapped resource for creating the kind of collaboration you need to excel.

- *Network-Actualized?* When both the individuals and the organization commit to their networker identities and when employees are trained and organizational systems support networking, then the organization's networking goals will be fully realized—and it will experience the growth and profitability that result when people collaborate to execute strategy, innovate, engage, and compete.

So, how do you, a leader, help your organization become Network-Actualized? By creating connections, sparking conversations, and fostering collaboration you can establish the conditions that are necessary for the Network-Oriented Workplace. Figure 9–2, Actions for Leaders, provides the outline for the rest of the chapter.

FIGURE 9–2. *Actions for Leaders*

Create Connections

What can happen when you connect the right people? Can you make face-to-face encounters more likely? Do people have time to connect? The answers to these questions reveal the actions you can take.

BRING STAKEHOLDERS TOGETHER

When Contacts Count polled 100 human resources managers, 91 said they saw a need to strategically manage the creation, maintenance, and growth of social capital in their organizations, yet 81 said their organizations did not have a well-defined, enterprise-wide strategy for developing the social capital of employees.

You can be the catalyst for creating that strategy. Bring together everyone who has a stake in developing the networking capabilities of employees, everyone whose initiatives will benefit as employees become more proficient and productive at networking. As you envision your team, think about including people from training and development, talent management, business development, sales, and marketing. Consider inviting people who manage innovation efforts, leadership development programs, orientation, employee resource groups, mentoring and diversity programs, and internal face-to-face or online networks. Who else do you need to get buy-in from? Who would be good champions? Whose expertise, such as corporate communications, do you need? The group that you have pulled together will be your KeyNet as you set your strategy and make your to-do list.

> *Be the catalyst for an enterprise-wide strategy for developing the social capital of employees.*

What will you say as you recruit people? What will the agenda for your first meeting need to include? Your KeyNet will be an example of the kind of collaboration that you want to encourage in your organization. Will coming together to work on ways to support networking be a simple task? That will depend on the attitude your organization currently has toward networking. If your organization is Discouraging, you may find the going tough; if it's Encouraging or Committed, you should have an easier time of it. The amount of time you'll need to spend will also depend on where you start. Think of this project as ongoing.

SYNC THE SYSTEMS

How will you align the infrastructure with your commitment to a networked, collaborative culture? This question will put lots of items on the KeyNet's agenda. Do we need to change our hiring policies, so that we attract people who already have a collaborative mindset? How about job descriptions and performance evaluations? Don't they need to mention networking? Do we need to adjust how people are compensated? Use your KeyNet's expertise to surface all of the areas you'll need to consider.

MAKE SPACE

In the book *Steve Jobs* by Walter Isaacson, Apple's cofounder says, "There's a temptation in our networked age to think that ideas can be developed by email and iChat. . . . That's crazy. Creativity comes from spontaneous meetings, from random discussions. You run into someone, you ask what they're doing, you say 'wow,' and soon you're cooking up all sorts of ideas."

Creating the physical environment in which these spontaneous meetings occur is something many organizations are already doing.

In February 2013, Yahoo's head of human resources Jackie Rees sent a memo to staff who had been working from home. It said in part, "To become the absolute best place to work, communication and collaboration will be important, so we need to be working side-by-side. That is why it is critical that we are all present in our offices. Some of the best decisions and insights come from hallway and cafeteria discussions, meeting new people, and impromptu team meetings. Speed and quality are often sacrificed when we work from home. We need to be one Yahoo, and that starts with physically being together." Working from home was cancelled.

What else can you do bring employees together?

· ·

How can your physical plant make connections happen?

· ·

Google's Bay View campus in California was designed to maximize what real estate head David Radcliffe calls, "casual collisions of the workforce." In an article in *Vanity Fair* magazine, Radcliffe says, "You can't schedule innovation. We want to create opportunities for people to have ideas and be able to turn to others right there and say, 'What do you think of this?'"

And what if your employees were encouraged to run into people outside the organization?

"Collisions" are also part of the vocabulary at Zappos, the online store. CEO Tony Hseih believes in setting the stage for casual contact. At the Las Vegas office, three entrances were blocked, making sure that employees bumped into each other at the one remaining. It is evident that the company prioritizes collisions over convenience. Hsieh also wanted his people to collide with business-people in the neighborhood. One of the closed entrances was at the end of the skywalk from the parking garage into the building. Employees were rerouted to sidewalks, a move that increased their chances for random encounters with people in the wider community. Hseih advises, ". . . meet lots of different people without trying to extract value from them. You don't need to connect the dots right away. But if you think about each person as a new dot on your canvas, over time, you'll see the full picture."

In hierarchical organizations, access to others was restricted, resulting in the walled-off departments or functions known as "silos" or "stovepipes." What can your KeyNet do to eliminate such barriers and promote connecting? How can you arrange your space so people will connect?

TAKE TIME

It's one thing to make the physical space conducive to connections, but do people have the time to stop and talk or will they pass on by? We call these times ChoicePoints—moments when people decide whether or not to interact. If people choose not to interact, what's to blame? Billable hours are the bugaboo in many firms. Productivity goals and tight deadlines hurry employees along. To take the time to connect, people will have to receive repeated reassurance that net-working is working. In the *Harvard Business Review* article, "IDEO's

Culture of Helping," the authors point out that a certain amount of "slack" in employees' schedules pays off and allows people to engage in unplanned ways.

> *Will employees stop and talk or will they pass on by?*

How can you provide time for networking? Can you increase the number of social events, volunteer projects, and sports activities to induce connections? And can you designate networking time at corporate gatherings?

Spark Conversation

As a leader, what can you do to refocus on the definition, raise the quality, and influence the content of conversation?

TALK "WITH" NOT "AT"

By definition, conversation is two-way. Moving from "command and control" to "connect and collaborate" means moving from monologues to dialogues. One kind of dialogue you as a leader can promote is the top-to-bottom kind of conversation: from management to employees.

Jack Stahl, former CEO of Revlon, Inc., and author of *Lessons on Leadership*, writes:

> A good leader spends significant time meeting and talking with people up, down, and across their organization. By being visible in this way, the leader is positioned to ask questions of his or her people to learn about their challenges, where they are struggling and any barriers to success. The leader can then provide coaching to those individuals and has the ability to help solve any systemic roadblocks that can prevent success for the larger organization. I found I can talk to over one hundred people per

week in one-on-one conversations simply by taking advantage of every opportunity to talk with people, before and after meetings, in the hallways, to and from the offices, and even in elevator conversations.

Note that Stahl's approach involves more than telling; it involves asking, listening, and coaching.

In their book, *Talk, Inc.*, Boris Groysberg and Michael Slind write, "A new source of organizational power has come to the fore. Our term for that power source is *organizational conversation*. Instead of handing down commands or imposing formal controls, many leaders today are interacting with their workforce in ways that call to mind an ordinary conversation between two people." Keeping those ideas in mind will help you have more valuable give-and-take conversations with employees.

Another kind of dialogue involves employees talking with one another. Once you've created the space and time for connection, you can home in on the quality of these exchanges.

IMPROVE THE QUALITY

Conversation in an organization improves as employees gain skill in asking questions and listening.

The bar is also raised when leaders "are fostering and facilitating conversation-like practices throughout their company—practices that enable a company to achieve higher degrees of trust, improved operational efficiency, greater motivation and commitment among employees, and better coordination between top-level strategy and frontline execution," say Groysberg and Slind in *Talk, Inc.* "The power of organizational conversation isn't the kind of power that manifests itself as control over a person or a process. Rather, it's the kind of power that makes a person or a process *go*. It's energy, in other words. It's fuel. In organizational terms, conversation is what keeps the engine of value creation firing on all cylinders."

In 1995, Juanita Brown and David Isaacs stumbled upon a conversation process. They went on to develop what's now called World Café. Organizations around the world use this free process. Yours can adopt it, too. See the website at www.theworldcafe.com for instructions.

Peter Senge of Massachusetts Institute of Technology's Sloan School of Management and author of *The Fifth Discipline* provides a testimonial: "World Café conversations are the most reliable way I have yet encountered for all of us to tap into collective creating. . . . I have been repeatedly struck by the ease of beginning a World Café–style dialogue—how readily people shift into heartfelt and engaging conversation."

How will you promote high-quality conversations?

TELL THE STORY

In the command-and-control environment, people tried to control the messages being sent from the organization to the outside world. Now, with the variety of communication technologies available to everyone, a cacophony of voices with a jumble of opinions and a mishmash of information—and misinformation—emanates from people inside your organization to those outside. There's no way to control that flow, but you can educate employees. One of the ways employees can impact your big issues is to tell your story—if they've learned it. The employee might be talking to potential clients or customers at a civic association meeting or to a neighbor who serves on the city council over the back fence. When people ask that employee, "What's new at YourCorp?" what's he going to say?

> *You can't control information flow, but you can educate employees.*

When we quizzed a group of employees about 10 of their firm's biggest achievements and latest news (taken directly from the firm's website), we found that people were aware of—and therefore could talk about—only 30 percent of their own company's successes.

In *Talk, Inc.*, the authors quote Andy Burris, VP of Corporate Marketing and Communications at McKesson Corporation. He says, "Ultimately, we would like to create a thirty-five thousand employee virtual sales force. . . . We aim to boost the level of business literacy throughout the organization. How do we make sure that someone in accounts payable knows enough to be dangerous? . . . If that person happens to be at a backyard barbecue with a neighbor who happens to be a physician, we want that person to know enough about what we offer to physician's practices that he or she can engage in meaningful conversation."

How can you increase the business literacy of your employees? And do you act as a role model, habitually finding and telling stories about your organization? Stories have staying power. They stick in the listeners' minds. They create a picture that can attract the best employees and clients. In today's organizations, storytelling is a skill everyone needs to master.

INSIST ON BRINGBACK

If you could look down on your organization from on high, what would the information flow look like? You've learned how you can influence the quality and accuracy of information flowing outward. How about increasing the inward flow of valuable business intelligence? We call that "BringBack." In command-and-control organizations, the battlements not only keep information from leaving, they also prevent information from entering. In the best companies, employees know that part of their role is to gather ideas from the outside world and give those ideas to their colleagues inside. Every day, legions of employees go to conferences, professional association meetings, civic events, and many other outside activities—usually at their organization's expense. How much money are you spending? What are you getting in return?

. . . .

BringBack is the inward flow of valuable business intelligence.

. . . .

In a 2013 *Associations Now* magazine article, "Intelligence by Design," author Kristin Clarke writes:

> The idea that intelligence gathering is everyone's business has infiltrated every staff level at the Consumer Electronics Association (CEA). . . . The culture was purposefully put in place by CEO Gary Shapiro, who has created what may be one of the most organized, robust internal intelligence-gathering and analysis systems within the association community.
>
> "If we're investing in having one of our employees travel, for instance, they know they're expected to go way beyond whatever their single purpose in going is," Shapiro says. "They always have a dual purpose—to gather intelligence on behalf of the association, to see how [something] is done elsewhere and come back and report on it." Sales staff in particular must share comprehensive written reports about what they've seen and heard which CEA summarizes and circulates widely across departments.

How can you significantly increase your organization's BringBack, so that you get a better ROI from networking and professional development events?

Foster Collaboration

Once you've made connections happen and raised conversation to the next level, you're ready for the final steps to collaboration: Paint the vision, invite employees to join in, and keep an eye on the progress.

KNOW YOUR LIMITS

You're not in command-and-control mode any more. You can't manage your employees' networks. In recent literature about collaborative and connected organizations tapping into the power of networks, there's great confusion about how leaders relate to these networks. We've seen other authors imply that leaders can and should be much more in control of the individual employee's networks than is desirable or even possible. Can leaders really "help employees develop and sustain" their networks? Can leaders really "align and direct" employee networks? Can leaders really "connect their employees to the right collaborators?" Should leaders really "remove people from" employee networks or "appoint network leaders?"

The answer to these questions is a resounding "No!" Each employee will manage his or her own networks. The minute you interfere in any of those ways, you turn networking into a job assignment. If, however, you provide training in trust-building and network-building skills, employees will know how to configure and use their networks to contribute the most to the organization. Of course, some people are going to be better at networking than other people—even after training—so do feel free to coach and mentor.

ANSWER "WHY?" AND "WHAT?"

Employees have two big questions: "Why should we collaborate?" and "Exactly what does collaboration look like?"

Simon Sinek, author of *Start with the Why* and popular TED Talk speaker, puts forward a very compelling argument that the most inspiring leaders, those that are able to get people to act towards achieving goals, start by answering the "Why?" question.

Coming up with the answer to "Why do we need to collaborate?" is part of your role as a leader. The more you can dramatize and illustrate the "Why," the more you'll be able to inspire your employees to action. You also might want to include a vivid description of the pain that can ensue when people don't collaborate. A huge and compelling example comes from the investigations after the terrorist attacks of 9/11. Investigators pointed a finger at the U.S. intelligence agencies for failing to collaborate and share information as one reason the attacks succeeded. The Australian bank executive revealing the $35 million cost of duplication is another supersize example. Don't rely just on examples from other organizations; show employees how collaboration—or the lack of it—will impact or has impacted your own organization. Your goal: Make sure employees "see" the benefits of collaboration clearly and "feel" the pain that absence of collaboration could bring. Answering "Why?" should give people a line of sight from what they are doing to what your organization is trying to achieve.

. . . .

Dramatize and illustrate the "Why?"

. . . .

1. *Why collaborate? To increase competitiveness.* It's Monday morning. The mood is somber. The partners of a mid-sized accounting firm listen to a report on the grim quarterly results. All statistics point to missed targets and another decline in revenues. They can no longer accept the trend as a temporary aberration. Something needs to change. How are they going to bring in the business? The group is asked for ideas. They give only rationalizations: "The economy is sluggish." "Our best clients are cutting back." They need new solutions . . . game changers . . . bold, courageous moves.

2. *Why collaborate? To execute strategy.* Sam, the project delivery manager in IT at a major bank, talks with his wife about the latest restructuring in the division. "It feels a bit like leaving New York on a Boeing 747 and having to rebuild the aircraft mid-flight and touchdown in London without losing any time," he says, shaking his head. To reduce costs, Sam has been told to lay off 60 percent of his U.S. employees and offshore their work to software engineers in India.

"How am I going to manage this change and still deliver the project by March?" Sam worries aloud. "The remaining people are struggling with their emotions. It's hard for them to see their friends go out the door. Not only that, they are going to have to work a lot harder as we go through this transition. And I'll be managing people I can't see, have never met, don't know the capabilities of, and who are in a different time zone and from a different culture." "So what are you going to do, Sam?" asks his wife. "I don't know," he says. "All I know is that my success will be based on how I execute this change and still deliver the project on time. Be prepared for me to be home a lot less."

3. *Why collaborate? To innovate.* At lunch in the cafeteria, a group of colleagues talks about the company's new product, 4TUNE. The marketing team's announcement enthusiastically promises that "this new game console will change the world," as anyone can use it to produce studio-quality music at home. Piggybacking on the popularity of music reality TV in Asia, the company is betting everything on a successful launch of 4TUNE there.

"Why did they keep this a secret for so long?" asks Jiro. "Anyone who has ever been to China will know that 4TUNE is destined to fail." "It's probably because the product development people don't expect anyone outside their closed circle to have an innovative idea in their brain," laughed Susan. "Well, I'm not going to say anything now. It's too late for that," chimed in Garima. "They obviously don't value the opinions of others in this company, so why bother?"

Tony listens with a puzzled look on his face. "You all are crazy. I think 4TUNE is very cool." Jiro responds, "4TUNE is indeed a cool piece of equipment, Tony. It's not the machine we objecting to; it's the name." Still puzzled, Tony says, "What do you mean?" "Well" says Jiro, "In China and in other Asian countries, the number 'four' is an inauspicious number. In fact, many buildings don't have a fourth floor . . . and if they do, it's usually vacant. People avoid using four, because it sounds like the word for death. That number in the name will stop people from buying the product."

4. *Why collaborate? To engage people.* The division head of a large financial services firm is pleased when Charlie sticks his head in the door and asks, "Have you got a minute?" He's one of her young and eager rising stars. He always has something valuable to share and always "tells it like it is." He sits down and slides a memo across her desk. She skims the top line: "It's with deep regret. . . ." Charlie says, "Bad news, I'm afraid. I am handing in my resignation. I've accepted a similar role with MetroBank." The division head is shocked. "Why Charlie?" she asks, almost pleading. He explains, "Look, I'm tired of begging for cooperation. I have trouble getting anything done. I want to work in an environment where there's more collaboration and camaraderie."

Answering the question "What does collaboration look like?" is just as important as explaining why collaboration is vital. There's no point in asking people to collaborate if they don't know exactly what behaviors that entails.

Use these three ways to highlight what collaboration really looks like.

1. Find examples in your own organization, no matter how small or local they might be. As you shine the spotlight on these efforts, you encourage others, even in different work areas, to use the same methods.

2. Find examples in your industry. Research association and trade publications to find out how others collaborate, so that you can publicize those ideas to people in your organization. Get in touch with successful collaborators and interview them to get tips. You could even bring in these people to talk at employee meetings.

3. Find examples through people in your ProNet. When Sondra went to her alumni meeting, she met Leon. Although she was in banking and he was in healthcare, she found that he had a wealth of good ideas for initiating more collaborative processes, especially when people were still learning how to build trust cross-functionally.

To show what collaboration is, tell the stories about how people are coming together to create new value: how they are saving the day, solving the problem, or serving the client. The collaborative organization must have a compelling collaborative vision.

ELICIT BUY-IN

Employees may understand the benefits and may have been trained in the skills, but you'll still need to get their buy-in. Note that the word "discretionary" appears in our definition of networking.

More than 30 years ago, Daniel Yankelovich and John Immerwahr, in their book *Putting the Work Ethic to Work*, described discretionary effort and its impact on organizational success. They defined it as the amount of effort individuals expend *over and above* the minimum they need to do to keep their jobs. Giving discretionary effort is a choice employees make. It can't be mandated by the organization. Even though networking may appear on people's job descriptions and may figure in their performance evaluations, it's still discretionary. Individual employees will decide, every day, whether they will take advantage of a ChoicePoint and stop and have a conversation in the hallway, for example. Leaders have been trying to tap into this discretionary effort for many decades. The 63 percent of employees who are "not engaged" are not exerting much discretionary effort.

· ·

Networking is a discretionary act.

· ·

A Network-Oriented Workplace is an environment in which people will choose to exert extra effort to share information, resources, support, and access to intentionally create new value with others inside and outside the organization. Why? It's a case of "riding the horse the way it's going." People are social animals; they build relationships. By training and inspiring them to do that better and more often, we help them take off at a gallop. It's easier to elicit incremental improvement than wholesale change.

MONITOR THE PROGRESS

As you're fostering a collaborative environment, you'll want to check on the progress. Figure 9–3, Getting to Collaboration, is a diagnostic flow chart to help you consider why collaboration might be stalled and to suggest actions you could take to get things moving.

Your KeyNet will find it helpful to ask these questions:

- *Will collaboration create value?* If the whole organization is committed to the Network-Oriented Workplace, the answer must be "yes." But that doesn't mean that every effort or task must involve collaboration. It's a tool to be used judiciously. Sometimes getting people to collaborate diminishes value by increasing costs and slowing down progress. If there is no value created, then don't waste your time. However, if there's evidence that value could be created by collaboration but collaboration remains low, then consider the next question.

- *Have you explained why collaboration is important?* If you've answered the "Why?" question effectively and showed how it fits (created the context) but collaboration remains low, then consider the next question.

- *Do your employees have the skills to collaborate?* If you have invested in training and coaching your people and they've reached a high level of competency but collaboration is still not happening, then consider the next question.

- *Are they aware that they are not collaborating?* Blind spots exist for both individuals and groups. As a leader, you can provide feedback to them, so that they are aware of their behavior. If you've provided feedback and collaboration is still low, consider the next question.

- *Does collaboration have negative consequences?* Sometimes there are hidden downsides to collaborating. You'll need to discover what they might be and eliminate them. If there are no negative consequences and collaboration remains low, then consider the next question.

FIGURE 9-3. *Getting to Collaboration*

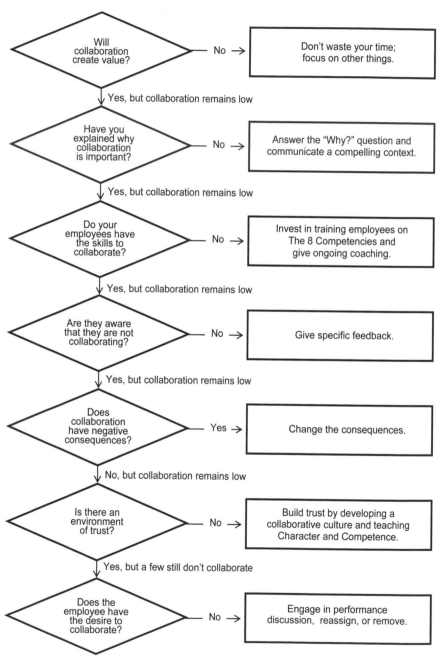

■ *Is there an environment of trust?* Trust is necessary for employee networks to develop to their full potential. Trust between employees can be destroyed by certain management actions, like downsizing, which pits employee against employee. To develop a networking culture means that not only do employees have the skills to teach and learn about each other's Character and Competence, but also that the environment doesn't value competition over collaboration. If there has been no disruption of trust and if employees have trust-building skills, then consider the next question.

■ *Does the employee have the desire to collaborate?* At the end of the day, you can create all the conditions for collaboration, and you may still find people who are resistant. Reassign them into jobs that demand less or no collaboration, give one-on-one performance coaching, or remove them from the organization.

As you move forward, continue to monitor and measure the impact of collaboration. Be sure to share success stories with employees to keep the enthusiasm high.

Your role as you take the lead in developing and supporting networking in your company is a big one. Your actions will include—but aren't limited to—the ones listed here. You'll find, we're sure, additional ways to create connections, spark conversations, and foster collaboration.

Organizations are floundering as the command-and-control mindset of the past breaks apart. Many are struggling to pull together a comprehensive view of managing in the new hyperconnected and collaborative workplace.

In 1960, management guru Douglas McGregor wrote in his groundbreaking book, *The Human Side of Enterprise*, "Fads will come and go. The fundamental fact of man's capacity to collaborate with his fellows in the face-to-face group will survive the fads and one day be recognized. Then, and only then, will management discover how seriously it has underestimated the true potential of its human resources."

Half a century later, you can help to realize this human potential through your strategic connections.

SUGGESTED READING

Baber, Anne, André Alphonso, and Will Kitchen. "Internal Networking: Time Waster or Value Creator." T+D magazine, American Society for Training & Development, October 2013.

Baber, Anne, and Lynne Waymon. "Career Insecurity." T+D magazine, American Society for Training & Development, June 2007.

Bhargava, Rohit. *Likeonomics: The Unexpected Truth Behind Earning Trust, Influencing Behavior, and Inspiring Action.* Hoboken, NJ: John Wiley & Sons, 2012.

Bryan, Lowell L., Eric Matson, and Leigh M. Weiss. "Harnessing the Power of Informal Employee Networks." *The McKinsey Quarterly*, November 2007.

Casciaro, Tiziana, and Miguel Sousa Lobo. "Competent Jerks, Lovable Fools and the Formation of Social Networks." *Harvard Business Review*, June 2005.

———. "When Competence Is Irrelevant: The Role of Interpersonal Affect in Task-Related Ties." *Administrative Science Quarterly*, December 2008.

Cross, Rob, Nitin Nohria, and Andrew Parker. "Six Myths About Informal Networks—and How to Overcome Them." *Harvard Business Review*, April 2002.

Davis, Jocelyn, Henry Frechette, and Edwin Boswell. *Strategic Speed: Mobilize People, Accelerate Execution.* Boston: Harvard Business Press, 2010.

Gladwell, Malcolm. *The Tipping Point.* Little, Brown Book Group Limited, 2000.

Gregerman, Alan. *The Necessity of Strangers: The Intriguing Truth About Insight, Innovation, and Success.* San Francisco: Jossey-Bass, 2013.

Grant, Adam. *Give and Take: A Revolutionary Approach to Success.* New York: Viking Adult, 2013.

Groysberg, Boris, and Michael Slind. *Talk, Inc.: How Trusted Leaders Use Conversation to Power Their Organizations*. Boston: *Harvard Business Review Press*, 2012.

Horn, Sam. *POP! Stand Out in Any Crowd*. New York: Penguin Books, 2006.

Hsieh, Tony. "Tony Hsiehs Rule for Success: Maximize Serendipity." http://www.inc.com/magazine/201302/rules-for-success/rule-2-tony-hsieh-maximize-serendipity.html

Huston, Larry, and Nabil Sakkab. "Connect and Develop." *Harvard Business Review*, March 2006.

"Leading Through Connections: 2012 IBM CEO Study." CEO C-suite Studies, 2012.

Lencioni, Patrick. *Silos, Politics, and Turf Wars*. San Francisco: Jossey-Bass, 2006.

Lovas, Michael, and Pam Holloway. *Axis of Influence: How Credibility and Likeability Intersect to Drive Success*. Garden City, NY: Morgan James Publishing, 2009.

Mauzy, Jeff, and Richard A. Harriman. *Creativity, Inc.: Building an Inventive Organization*. Boston: Harvard Business School Publishing, 2003.

Maxwell, John C. *The 360° Leader: Developing Your Influence from Anywhere in the Organization*. Nashville, TN: Nelson Word, 2006.

Nowak, Achim. *Infectious: How To Connect Deeply and Unleash The Energetic Leader Within*. New York: Allsworth Press, 2012.

Schrage, Michael. *No More Teams—Mastering the Dynamics of Creative Collaboration*. New York: Currency Doubleday, 1995.

Sinek, Simon. *How Great Leaders Inspire Action*. www.ted.com, 2009.

Stahl, Jack. *Lessons on Leadership: The 7 Fundamental Management Skills for Leaders at All Levels*. New York: Kaplan Publishing, 2007.

Stallard, Michael Lee. *The Connection Culture: A New Source of Competitive Advantage*. E-book, 2008.

Waymon, Lynne and André Alphonso. "Who Trusts You? The Key to Attracting Advocates." *The Marketer*, Society of Marketing Professional Services, February 2014.

Waymon, Lynne, André Alphonso, and Pamela Bradley. "Raising Rainmakers." *The Journal of Accountancy*, American Institute of CPAs, May 2014.

"Why Good Strategies Fail: Lessons for the C-Suite." A Report from the Economist Intelligence Unit. *The Economist*, March 2013.

INDEX

ABOUT THE AUTHORS

Baber, Waymon, Alphonso, and **Wylde** are collaborators at Contacts Count LLC, an international training and consulting firm that specializes in business networking.

Their unique approach uses The 8 Competencies for the Network-Oriented Workplace™ to help clients profit from the changes facing organizations that are moving from a command-and-control mode to a more participative and engaged way of working. Contacts Count's training programs, keynotes, workshops, and webinars show organizations how to harness the power of individual employee networks to impact enterprise-wide goals such as strategy execution, innovation, engagement, and competitiveness.

Anne Baber and **Lynne Waymon**, of Newtown, Pennsylvania, cofounded the firm 24 years ago and are the coauthors of seven earlier books that help people put the tools of networking to work in the service of business goals. *Make Your Contacts Count: Networking Know-How for Business and Career Success*, now in its second edition, has been a best seller in the business and career world.

André Alphonso, based in Sydney, manages Contacts Count's business in Australia, India, and Asia. He has more than 30 years of business and consulting experience and specializes in training and organizational development. André has held executive-level positions with Forum Corporation and Unisys.

Jim Wylde, of Arlington, Virginia, is an organizational development specialist, a leadership coach, an experienced facilitator, and a seasoned Certified Contacts Count Trainer. He works with U.S. and international audiences. Jim speaks Spanish and holds a degree in international affairs with concentrations in Latin American studies and international development.

Contacts Count's clients include corporations such as Lockheed Martin, Booz Allen, and eBay; professional services firms such as KPMG, Sapient, and Keiter CPA; universities such as Georgetown, University of Arizona, and George Washington; associations such as The Society of Women Engineers and the American Society for Training and Development (now the Association for Talent Development); and numerous government agencies such as NASA, the U.S. Department of State, and the National Institutes of Health.

Contacts Count's training and consulting services help organizations and individuals build strategic, trust-based relationships that get the job done, boost profits, and expand influence in the Network-Oriented Workplace. The firm licenses organizations to deliver their material internally and leads in-house train-the-trainer certification programs.

Contacts Count welcomes your comments and inquiries through their website at www.ContactsCount.com.